Praise for *The New World of Wireless*

"Most techniques for modeling the future are backward-looking. They utilize past data in attempts to see what's up ahead. Although such an approach remains useful, *The New World of Wireless* is about a different approach to modeling the future. Scott Snyder introduces the reader to the forward-looking technique of scenario planning and applies it to the rapidly changing world of technology. Scenario planning is not about predicting the future, but rather identifying the forces and constraints around which multiple future worlds may flow. Snyder is an excellent thinker, and shows in reasonable terms how the strategist can create extremely long-term plans while remaining grounded in reality. This book is less about prediction and more about possibilities."

—**Mark Pecen**, Vice President, Research In Motion, Limited

"You may disagree with Dr. Snyder's assessment of the future, but if you are involved in business or public policy, you would be foolish to ignore it. There is no question we have been—and continue to be—attacked by an intensifying digital swarm. Dr. Snyder's book provides deep insight into its consequences. At best he is correct; at worst he forces the reader to develop his/her own views of what lies ahead. There are no facts in the future, but this book certainly lays out a well-written, well-thought-out, high-probability scenario that must be assessed and planned for. I, for one, agree with Dr. Snyder's analysis and highly recommend his book."

—**Edmond Thomas**, partner, Harris, Wiltshire & Grannis LLP and former Chief Engineer of the Federal Communications Commission

"Scott Snyder helps us see around the corner of wireless technology—no mean feat. He explains why advances in 4G and beyond will profoundly change the way we play, work, and live. Managers ignore digital swarms at their peril, especially the killer-bee scenario that will more than sting. Major shifts will emerge in markets, business models, and indeed society after digital swarms start to buzz. Snyder shows you how to catch the wave rather than be washed ashore, using clear examples, compelling arguments, intriguing scenarios, and sound business advice. I highly recommend this book."

—**Paul J. H. Schoemaker**, PhD, The Wharton School, author of *Winning Decisions*, *Profiting from Uncertainty*, and *Peripheral Vision*

"Snyder's book provides a thought-provoking look into the 4G future. While technical details abound, the importance of this work relates more to the social, business, and political implications of 4G technology. Snyder has provided us a glimpse of how different our lives will be in the not-so-distant future, and done so with amazing insight. It is truly a must-read."

—**Stanton Sloane**, PhD, CEO, SRA International

"*The New World of Wireless* is an impressive, thoughtful journey that helps business leaders see over the horizon to our unwired future, where we belong."

—**John Chen**, Chairman, CEO, and President, Sybase, Inc.

The New World
of Wireless

The New World of Wireless

How to Compete in
the 4G Revolution

Scott Snyder

(handwritten) 1030737

APR 2 7 2010

Vice President, Publisher: Tim Moore
Associate Publisher and Director of Marketing: Amy Neidlinger
Wharton Editor: Steve Kobrin
Editorial Assistant: Pamela Boland
Development Editor: Russ Hall
Operations Manager: Gina Kanouse
Senior Marketing Manager: Julie Phifer
Publicity Manager: Laura Czaja
Assistant Marketing Manager: Megan Colvin
Cover Designer: Alan Clements
Managing Editor: Kristy Hart
Project Editor: Anne Goebel
Copy Editor: Gayle Johnson
Proofreader: Apostrophe Editing Services
Indexer: Lisa Stumpf
Senior Compositor: Jake McFarland
Manufacturing Buyer: Dan Uhrig

Pearson Education LTD.
Pearson Education Australia PTY, Limited.
Pearson Education Singapore, Pte. Ltd.
Pearson Education North Asia, Ltd.
Pearson Education Canada, Ltd.
Pearson Educación de Mexico, S.A. de C.V.
Pearson Education—Japan
Pearson Education Malaysia, Pte. Ltd.

Library of Congress Cataloging-in-Publication Data

Snyder, Scott A. (Scott Andrew), 1965-

The new world of wireless : how to compete in the 4G revolution / Scott A. Snyder.

p. cm.

ISBN-13: 978-0-13-700379-2 (hardback : alk. paper)

ISBN-10: 0-13-700379-X (hardback : alk. paper)

1. Wireless communication systems--Social aspects. 2. Wireless communication systems--Economic aspects. 3. Wireless communication systems--Forecasting. 4. Interpersonal communication--Technological innovations--Social aspects. 5. Interpersonal communication--Technological innovations--Economic aspects. I. Title.

TK5103.2.S657 2009

658.8'72--dc22

2009007458

This book is dedicated to my own personal swarm—
Carson, Evan, Lindsey, Morgan, and especially
Susan—for being always connected to me, physically,
emotionally, and virtually. They are my constant
source of energy and inspiration.

Contents

Foreword

We are rapidly approaching the fifth wave of the Information Technology revolution that has changed how people work, play, and communicate. The mainframe wave of the 1950s, '60s, and '70s created the first widely available electronic version of information that had historically been kept in ledgers, filing cabinets, and binders. The minicomputer wave of the 1970s and '80s extended this analog-to-digital trend beyond the finance and research functions at the head office to include the shop floor and regional offices. Personal computers in the 1980s and '90s made more of this information available to the individual while thankfully replacing typewriters, calculators, and "foils" for all of us. Finally, the networking wave of the 1990s and 2000s connected these islands of data and processing power through local and wide area networks and, ultimately, the Internet.

The mobility wave now in play may have the most profound impact of all. While the previous waves were built on computers that communicate, mobility represents a completely new model: communication devices that compute. Power is shifting from centrally controlled information toward a future where individuals are empowered to compute, communicate, and collaborate in a way that best meets their needs. The mainframe, minicomputer, PC, and networking waves focused on making the corporation more efficient, with very little thought of making the individual more powerful. That is about to change.

In the mobility era, the traditional hierarchy is being flipped on its head. Enterprise-out no longer works. Expectations are being rewritten. For example, the under-40 segment of the world's population has grown up believing that phone numbers are for people, not places. They do not accept that the price tag on an item is the market price. They make decisions in real time with input from both known (their social networks) and unknown (Google) sources. They keep in touch with a far larger group of people than their parents did. They blur the lines between work, play, and communications constantly, with no need to be "unplugged" at any point in their day.

Beyond the generation gap, entire regions of the developing world have simply skipped ahead to a more productive, empowered, and entertaining way of working and living. Wired phone lines and fixed broadband Internet access will never achieve the penetration rates seen in the developed world, because people have gone directly to mobile and are not coming back.

Collectively, this is the Digital Swarm at work. We got the first glimpse of mobility's potential in the task workers of developed economies during the early 2000s. Seventy percent of workers in these countries require mobility because they do not sit at a desk. Companies such as Symbol Technologies produced rugged mobile devices for all those nurses, truck drivers, and first responders to bring information to the point of business activity. In many ways, we were in the clipboard replacement business. The mobile device became the eyes and ears of the enterprise, providing real-time information about the prescription a patient was receiving; the loading dock a pallet was delivered to; and the battle plan for police, fire, and security personnel during natural disasters.

However, this stage of mobility was still very much enterprise-out. The mobile devices were corporate assets and spent the night in their charging cradles at work. Mobility is now transforming beyond these humble beginnings, driven by more advanced devices such as the iPhone, widely available broadband cellular, and WiFi, and dramatic changes in how individuals are using mobile voice, data, pictures, and video personally and professionally.

Scott Snyder brings a visionary and thoughtful perspective to what the impact of this Digital Swarm will be and how your organization must realign its strategy to prosper in the age of mobility. He introduces insightful scenarios for how mobility will evolve and how discontinuous this fifth wave of IT will be. Set-and-forget strategies simply will not work. Winning in the Digital Swarm will require you to constantly assess changes in your customers' expectations, competitive set, and business model. It will place a premium on set-and-reset approaches to business strategy and execution.

The good news is that the inflection points between waves of information technology have always provided opportunities for aggressive, innovative companies to emerge as the new leaders. At the same time, the old guard will either fall by the wayside, like Digital Equipment Corporation, or reinvent themselves, like IBM. In your industry, which will you be?

—**Todd Hewlin**, Managing Partner of TCG Advisors

Acknowledgments

I would like to acknowledge several people who were influential in helping me write this book.

First, I would like to thank progressive thinkers in the wireless communications space such as Mark Pecen from RIM, Doug Smith from Clearwire, and Shoshi Loeb from Telcordia for our provocative interactions over the last several years. Your foresight around wireless is much appreciated and has certainly shaped my thinking in this book. I would especially like to thank Mark Pecen for providing a rich historic perspective on the wireless revolution and debunking some of the performance claims for 3G and 4G technologies.

Second, I would like to thank my colleagues at DSI for being so supportive when I was writing this book. With their help, I have learned the power of scenario planning as a method to challenge current assumptions and search for innovation opportunities. In particular, I would like to thank Paul Schoemaker, who has been both a role model and mentor in bringing breakthrough ideas and methodologies to the market through his writing. Thanks to Paul's encouragement, I pursued my passion to write a unique book on the future intersections between wireless and business.

Last, I would like to thank all the students I have been fortunate enough to have in my graduate courses at the University of Pennsylvania. They have been a great source of spirited debate, fresh perspectives, and new ideas related to what is possible with advanced communications technology. Many of these students have gone on to leverage wireless innovations in both large corporations and start-up businesses.

It is always gratifying to see theory translate into practice.

About the Author

Dr. Scott Snyder brings a unique mix of thought leadership in next-generation wireless systems and adaptive business strategy. He is currently the CEO of Decision Strategies International, a leading management consulting firm focused on scenario-based strategic planning and decision making. He is also a senior fellow in the Management Department at the Wharton School and an adjunct faculty member in the School of Engineering and Applied Science at the University of Pennsylvania. He has lectured extensively on emerging fourth-generation wireless networks and business models, telecommunications and IT strategy, and product development. He holds a patent for online decision aids and has been quoted as a thought leader in numerous publications, including the *Los Angeles Times*, *The Wall Street Journal*, *Phone +*, the *Philadelphia Inquirer*, and the *Philadelphia Business Journal*. Dr. Snyder earned his BS, MS, and PhD in systems engineering from the University of Pennsylvania and has an executive degree from USC in telecommunications management.

Dr. Snyder has more than 20 years of experience in business leadership, strategic planning, decision support systems, and technology management for both Fortune 500 companies and start-up ventures. Dr. Snyder has held executive positions with several Fortune 500 companies, including GE, Martin Marietta, and Lockheed Martin. He has also started business ventures in software, including Omni-Choice, a CRM/Analytics software applications provider, where he served as CTO and CEO. He was a candidate for Entrepreneur of the Year for the Philadelphia Region. He has worked with numerous Fortune 500 clients on business and technology strategy, including GE, CVS, AT&T, Sprint, Cingular, Accenture, NCR, Verizon, Echostar, Exelon, Microsoft, DuPont, Lockheed Martin, ConocoPhillips, National Grid, Siemens, and Scholastic. He also has worked with government organizations such as the U.S. Navy, FAA, DoD, DARPA, DLA, NASA, and NSA.

Introduction

When I was 14, I remember meeting some friends in a small nearby town to hang out and do something unproductive like checking out girls. By the time I got there, a few of my friends had beaten me to the punch, deciding to go to the local movie theater with a few girls they had met. Because I didn't know this, I searched frantically for them, cursing them under my breath. Just as I was ready to phone my mom from the corner pay phone, they strutted up with big grins on their faces. After unloading on them with a few expletives, I calmed down, and we grabbed a slice of pizza and a soda. The girls were gone, and I asked if my friends had gotten their numbers. They said, "Uh, we forgot to ask," and I began to question the intelligence of the guys I was hanging out with. We called my mom from the pay phone in the pizza place to ask her to pick us up. She gave me an earful because she had just been into town and would now have to drive back. I was thinking how I couldn't wait to be old enough to drive.

If I fast-forward 30 years and think about being a 14-year-old today (I have one of these creatures), here is how this same story might read. I decided to meet some friends in a nearby town after we exchanged text messages. When I got there (yes, my mom still would have driven me), I did not see my friends at our regular meeting spot, so I jumped on my mobile phone's "buddy beacon" to show where they were on a Google street map. I saw that they were at the movie theater, so I started walking in that direction. Meanwhile, I checked the local movie listings online and was happy to see that two new movies were showing that I wanted to see. In addition, I noticed a new message on my Facebook site. A girl I had met a week before, Shannon, was headed into town and wanted to see me. I shot her back a text to meet me at the movies. We got there at the same time and walked into the lobby, where my friends were standing with some girls I didn't recognize. We all went into the theater and immediately added each other to our Facebook lists and exchanged music and video libraries. I noticed on her site that one of the girls went to a private school with my sister. By the time we finished the movie and had our pizza, I was connected to no fewer than 50 new "friends" through exchanging social nets with the new girls we had met via our cell phones. Shannon had to leave, so we agreed to exchange ideas on the next place to meet via Facebook (sounded like a date!). Meanwhile, I checked my mom's beacon and saw that she was still parked in town, and I texted her to let her know we needed a ride home. She shot back a note that said, "Good thing you caught me." And I was still wishing I could drive sooner.

The difference in these stories is pretty dramatic. Yet because of the relatively small incremental changes each day, we fail to see how much wireless has changed our lives and is embedded in everything we do. Changing the scenario just described into professionals and organizations, and replacing the teenagers with knowledge workers in a mobile sales force, project team, or R&D group, we are starting to witness the same dramatic changes in how we work with wireless as a key enabler. President Obama demanding to keep his BlackBerry is a testament to the new model of work and life in the unwired world!

If we think ahead to the next decade, the changes driven by wireless could be even more significant as new technologies are deployed and users continue to innovate at an accelerating pace. The most dramatic changes will be in how people, devices, and other objects self-organize to carry out coordinated activities as distributed groups with intelligent devices using wireless as a collaboration and decision-making platform. We will call this organic group behavior among empowered wireless users and objects the "Digital Swarm." As opposed to popular terms like "convergence," "interconnectedness," and "pervasiveness," which focus primarily on information networks, Digital Swarm captures the added behavioral dimension that will be fundamental in shaping the unwired future. Not only will the Digital Swarm change our lives as consumers, but it will also transform how we do business. This shift could be even more dramatic than the disruptions created by the Internet or biotech revolutions over the last decade, because it truly lives at the intersection of human behavior and technology.

To date, most organizations and their leaders have failed to take advantage of wireless technology to create value in their business. While consumers have set a blistering pace of innovation around wireless applications such as location-based services, e-wallet, mobile entertainment, wireless social networking, and health monitoring, businesses continue to deploy wireless as little more than an extended communications medium and productivity tool. This gap will become more acute as the next generation of wireless technologies are deployed, called fourth generation, or 4G. Not only will 4G increase the performance of current wireless systems, but it also will shift the paradigm to user-centric networks and applications, with the user's device becoming the remote control for all activities. 4G will be the technology enabler for the Digital Swarm, where collective action is decentralized and self-organizing, with no boundaries, no control, and no barriers to innovation by users.

While big companies and their CIOs try to reign in unapproved devices and applications like the iPhone and Gmail, the new wireless wave is building, ready to crash down on markets, companies, and employees. Rather than brace against it, organizations must swim ahead by creating the skills, capabilities, and mindset to leverage it. Those that do will be rewarded with significant innovation and value creation. Those that don't will be swept away with the tide, because they will be ill-equipped to compete in the new unwired playing field.

The New World of Wireless is written for business leaders and managers hoping to anticipate and leverage the next wireless wave to their advantage. With the exception of a handful of past wireless innovators like FedEx and the U.S. military, and upstart models such as Helio, MeshNetworks, and Fon, most organizations have failed to capture the full potential of today's wireless networks and devices, because almost all wireless innovation has been driven by the consumer sector. Yet we are about to see a major shift in the current wireless services model, creating disruption across the entire value chain with distributed, self-organizing wireless users gaining more primary control over future services and how they deliver value. This shift will present a unique opportunity for companies with the right skills and culture to innovate and create profit opportunities around these new platforms. It will also threaten to cripple businesses that are too rigid and hierarchical to shift the power of decisions and experimentation to the edge of their business.

This book presents a new framework, WiQ (wireless IQ), for measuring your organization's wireless readiness and assessing the potential business impact of the social, technological, economic, and political forces that are shaping the future of wireless. Tremendous value will be created and destroyed as this new and very chaotic unwired future unfolds. This book will challenge your current mindsets and business models against the possible unwired future and will identify the success strategies needed to create true competitive advantages from the Digital Swarm.

Although books have been written about current wireless networks (second- and third-generation cellular) and future wireless networks (4G), they have been technology-centric. They pay very little attention to the broader strategic and organizational context for businesses using these technologies. In fact, there is consensus that the business sector has been a laggard as a whole in adopting and leveraging wireless technology when compared to the consumer sector, where innovation is rampant. Is this because organizations lack the skills and structure to take advantage of wireless or that the networks themselves do not offer enough value to justify the investment? As the wireless paradigm shifts to users being at the center of the network, companies can ill afford not to innovate as their customers, partners, and employees become empowered by the Digital Swarm.

There are also many books on innovation and breakthrough strategies. However, none of these focuses on the enormous power of wireless as a platform for innovation. While "business without wires" is happening in incremental ways, there is not enough thinking about what an unwired business could truly enable. Aart de Geus, CEO of Synopsys, says "Increasing computing power in cell phones creates unlimited mobility and unlimited space in which interactivity can take place. This is an amazing combination, and we have not yet seen the full fruits of it." The timing of this book is ideal, because new signals of 4G disrupting markets and companies are appearing everywhere. As this book was being written, sales of iPhones had exceeded 30 million, and Google's Android operating system had just been released; both are early examples of 4G cognitive devices. While companies and their employees see the change happening, they continue to react instead of adapting their organizations to take advantage of it. WiQ gives them a framework to assess their organizational gaps and identify investments to profit from the 4G wave.

The New World of Wireless fills an important need by addressing wireless innovation with the business executive in mind. By doing so, it could kick off an entire wave of transformational thinking around this emerging and highly disruptive area.

This book integrates several conceptual frameworks to interpret and assess the business impact of the emerging unwired future. These are the primary frameworks used:

- **Environmental scanning/trend scouting** to identify early signals of change and potential tipping points for emerging wireless technologies and business models
- **Systems thinking**, including Causal Influence Mapping,[1] to identify both obvious and nonobvious interactions among key drivers in shaping the unwired future
- **Scenario planning** to depict alternative futures that help frame different possible social, economic, political, and technological uncertainties around wireless[2]

- **Innovation methods**, including Disruptive Innovation[3] and Innovation Networks, to spot both eroding and winning business models
- **Strategic options generation and evaluation** to capture the upsides and effectively manage the downsides[4] of new wireless opportunities

The new conceptual frameworks and tools developed in the book are as follows:

- The identification of key drivers and representative scenarios to inform business decision-making and strategy around next-generation wireless.
- A new organizational assessment tool, WiQ, to determine wireless readiness for a given organization and strategic environment. Over 50 business leaders were surveyed for wireless need and readiness as part of developing the WiQ assessment tool.
- A foundational model for creating new business and product innovations using wireless.
- An adaptive strategy and decision-making framework for creating sustainable competitive advantage as the unwired future unfolds.

By leveraging existing frameworks and introducing new ones, this book provides managers with a broad "toolkit" for navigating the unwired future to create a competitive advantage for your organization. The book's structure, as shown in Figure I.1, is built around four key objectives:

- **Understanding** the changes happening in wireless that matter to your business
- **Interpreting** how these changes will affect your organization and market
- **Innovating** around new wireless opportunities to create a competitive advantage for your business
- **Transforming** your business to harness the Digital Swarm

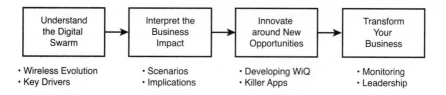

Figure I.1 This book's key objectives

Following this structure, the book starts by describing the Digital Swarm and what got us there. **Chapter 1, "The Swarm Analogy and the Wireless Revolution,"** defines the Digital Swarm and looks at the patterns of evolution in wireless that have positioned us for a new revolution. **Chapter 2, "Digital Swarm Drivers,"** provides current and emerging examples of the Digital Swarm and identifies the ten social, technological, economic, political, and environmental forces that will drive the Digital Swarm. The next several chapters establish a future view of where the Digital Swarm could go and its wide-reaching effects. **Chapter 3, "Possible Future Scenarios: Convergence, Collision, Confluence,"** presents two possible extreme scenarios for the unwired future developed from the drivers and themes identified in previous chapters. The implications of these alternative unwired futures are examined for individuals, organizations, industries in different regions of the world in **Chapter 4, "The Swarm Effect: Implications for You and Your Company."** The next two chapters identify strategies for success and wireless innovation opportunities in the future. **Chapter 5, "Organizing for Success: Strategies and Options,"** describes success strategies needed for companies to thrive in the new unwired environment and presents the WiQ assessment tool. **Chapter 6, "Monitoring and Adapting to Early Signals,"** talks about specific innovation opportunities that may be enabled by the Digital Swarm and staked out by early adopters. The final two chapters discuss how to create an organization that can adapt and win in the Digital Swarm. **Chapter 7, "Killer Swarm Apps,"** discusses how companies can monitor new changes and develop an adaptive strategy for sustaining a competitive advantage in the highly dynamic wireless future. **Chapter 8, "Swarm Leadership,"** summarizes the "stuff that matters" and proposes a leadership agenda to win in the Digital Swarm. **Appendix A, "Taking the WiQ Survey,"** is the WiQ Executive Survey. **Appendix B, "Wireless 101: Inside the Technology,"** is an in-depth technical overview of wireless systems in case you want to venture further into that topic.

Given the dramatic changes we have experienced so far and can expect in the future as a result of wireless technology, this book is much more the start of a journey than an endpoint. As such, the references to specific technologies and players reflect the environment at the time this book was written. Inevitably, these examples will evolve and be replaced by a new wave of examples. However, the persistent, disruptive pace of wireless and the shift to the new Digital Swarm paradigm should be a constant, no matter what scenario we end up in. Charting your own course is both the challenge and the opportunity presented by the Digital Swarm.

1

The Swarm Analogy and the Wireless Revolution

"If you're looking for a role model in a world of complexity, you could do worse than to imitate a bee."

—*Thomas Seely, bee expert*

Swarms have existed since the beginning of the Earth among various types of species, from insects, to fish, to birds. More recently, "swarm intelligence" has been applied to everything from airplane gate routing by Southwest Airlines to guerilla marketing with "swarmteams."[1]

The Merriam-Webster definition of a swarm is a large number of animate or inanimate things massed together and usually in motion.

If you think of wireless networks as connecting a virtual mass of users and networked objects, allowing them to converge around specific places, ideas, or activities in a semicoordinated fashion, this is, in fact, a swarm. This is a concept beyond the "convergence," "interconnectedness," and "pervasiveness" we have seen in information networks. Not only are swarms interconnected and pervasive, they also include a collective behavior and purpose that is not captured in these other concepts. It is this underlying characteristic that also makes it so difficult for organizations to see the early signals of this new paradigm. Figure 1.1 shows a number of wireless technologies and social networking that enable swarms among networked users, much like the coordinated activities of bees around a hive.

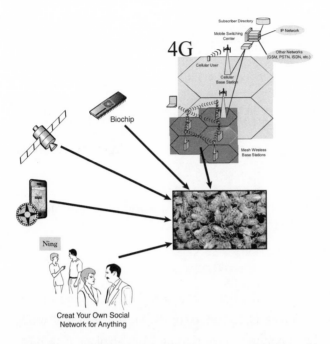

Figure 1.1   Wireless technologies and social networking enable swarms among networked users.

Wirelessly enabled swarms have occurred in recent years, such as the throngs of disgruntled citizens in the Philippines who tried to take over government buildings using text messaging to coordinate their movements.[2] However, the current wireless networks do not support "swarming" as a natural occurrence due to limitations in interoperability, location awareness, device intelligence, and capacity. The newest fourth generation of wireless technology, or 4G, overcomes these limitations, opening the possibility of swarming as a routine occurrence in both professional and social situations. (The three previous wireless generations will be defined later in this chapter.)

Value Proposition

Here's why your company needs to understand and turn information about the Digital Swarm to your financial advantage:

- Wireless is now embedded in everything we do.
- This will significantly disrupt companies and markets.

- Organizations need to adapt quickly to create a competitive advantage and avoid being blindsided.

You will explore four key questions:

- What is happening in wireless that you need to know about?
- How could this play out in the marketplace?
- How will it impact your organization?
- What can you do to position for success?

First, let's try to define 4G wireless, the catalyst for the Digital Swarm, to the best extent possible, given that it is still a fuzzy, evolving collection of technologies and concepts. Several potential 4G standards are emerging, including WiMax and LTE (Long-Term Evolution). However, the commonly accepted goals are that 4G will allow typical users to get over 100 megabits per second (Mbps) to their wireless device anywhere they go. This is more than their home broadband connection and even more than a large office building does today. Users also would have smart devices that can provide the most appropriate services based on their "presence" or specific situation. This would allow 4G users to download HD movies in seconds; engage in virtual-reality business and entertainment applications; and get real-time, rich media related to their unique context and location. Sounds appealing, to say the least!

But 4G is just an enabler. The intersection of this technology platform with other social, economic, political, and technological effects will enable the Digital Swarm.

Key Insight

4G wireless will marry incredibly high speeds anywhere you go with contextual awareness to create an immersive, "user-centric" wireless experience.

A Day in the 4G Life

"Chaos in the world brings uneasiness, but it also allows the opportunity for creativity and growth."
—*Tom Barrett, author*

Close your eyes. Imagine yourself sitting in your home or office with streams of information moving between you and the objects around you. Actions take place in your immediate environment as you orchestrate them from your mobile device. Only relevant information is sent to you as your personal "bot" negotiates and filters massive streams of data on your behalf. Your interactions with other people take the form of abstract transmissions of ideas that you exchange in real time as if they were immediate. Instead of using archaic serial communications, you can interact with several of their virtual profiles in parallel to have several conversations at once. Your device is constantly aware of your condition because your health and emotions are monitored systematically via the personal network that constantly surrounds your body. The distinction between life and work has become blurred across a continuum of time and space where decisions are made, and actions are taken to optimize both performance and personal satisfaction. You can easily immerse yourself into both real and simulated situations via high-definition digital media for both work and play. You have become a biological networked appliance who can link to the global communications grid anytime and anywhere. Like others who can afford the best technology, you have complete awareness and control whenever you need it. This is your new way of life.

Now open your eyes. This may seem like fantasy, but the notion of individuals sensing and controlling their environment without depending on the infrastructure that surrounds us today is not far off. Advances in wireless technology, distributed computing, artificial intelligence, and biotechnology are laying the foundation for a new world and society without wires. As technology drives deeper into the human experience, a new world is beginning to emerge that we need to acknowledge and reconcile with our current assumptions. The idea of individuals self-organizing to act in a way that results in the most efficient and effective outcomes is certainly appealing. But this also raises some fundamental questions about what society would be like under these "swarmlike" conditions. There are even more practical questions about how business will be conducted and how companies will organize in this very distributed world:

- Where will the intersections of technology and social effects create tipping points for new killer applications?
- What will be the price of the information required to enable optimal decisions? Will it be at the expense of privacy or wealth?
- Who will monitor, organize, and control the individuals making the self-directed decisions? And how will the actions of these individuals be governed?
- Will companies become slaves to the actions of those who work there, or will they be able to harness the power of the "intelligent mob" to unlock significant new levels of innovation and performance?

Key Insight

The Digital Swarm will be shaped more by how people use next-generation wireless technology than the technology itself.

In the movie *Spider-Man*, Peter Parker's Uncle Ben tells him, "With great power comes great responsibility." Will society and individuals be able to harness the power they are given by the Digital Swarm, or will it overwhelm them? In this book, we will journey into the future unwired world and explore some of the scenarios that may unfold, and the implications for individuals, companies, and society as a whole. The images of this new world may also present some deep challenges to our current assumptions and beliefs. We must confront them if we are to succeed and thrive in the future Digital Swarm.

The Path to the 4G Wireless Era

"Cellular radio is not so much a new technology as a new idea
for organizing existing technology on a larger scale."
—*George Calhoun, author*

Just as many of us are getting up to speed on our 3G phones and
what they can do, buzz is already starting to develop around 4G wireless. 1G, 2G, 3G, 4G, WiFi, WiMax. Is this just technobabble, or do
you really need to be aware of these? My answer is an emphatic *yes*,
especially given the less-than-stellar track record of both individuals
and companies at anticipating the impact of technology on our lives
and organizations. We do not have to look back very far to see where
the best "experts" missed the signals of change or possibly even over-
valued them for an emerging technology area. Many technologies
take years before they have a significant impact on markets or consumers. It took almost three decades before the Internet's potential
to disrupt the retail market was realized, as shown in Figure 1.2. Yet
along the road are many carcasses of companies that overinvested in
what they thought was a "sure thing" during the Internet bubble, only
to find out that consumers weren't ready to change.

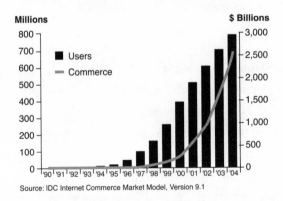

Source: IDC Internet Commerce Market Model, Version 9.1

Figure 1.2   The delayed payoff of e-commerce[3]

Another example is biotechnology, where the promise of genomics-based medicine has been around for many years. DNA was discovered in 1953, and the first gene sequencing was done in 1972. Yet the mapping of the Human Genome was not completed until over 30 years later, in 2003. The biotech industry reached $23 billion in 2000, rising to $50 billion in 2005 despite $350 billion invested.[4] Many unexpected social, political, and technical hurdles caused biotech to take much longer than expected to deliver significant benefit to the healthcare market. Many investors, including governments, placed a lot of chips on the promise of genetically engineered drugs, only to find out that they were not ready for prime time.

Key Insight

Emerging technologies are hard to predict. Missing the important signals increases the chance that we will get blindsided or overreact.

Much like the delayed payoff of e-commerce and the market impact of biotechnology, the evolution of wireless has been hard to predict. Back in 1947, when the first cellular concept was proposed at Bell Labs, no one could have imagined the global wireless revolution that would be sparked decades later by this new technology. As with lots of other nascent technologies, large players, such as the FCC and AT&T, failed to see the potential, as evidenced by the following account:

> "First, AT&T underestimated how important wireless communications would become. At the time of the break-up in 1984, AT&T relied on a report by McKinsey, a consultancy company, which claimed there would be fewer than 1 million wireless phone users by 2000. In fact, there were 740 million. Cellular technology was then spotty—calls were often lost, the signal short and the power used by devices high—so AT&T declined to enter this small market. Until, that is, 1994, when it paid $11.5 billion for McCaw Cellular, which became AT&T Wireless and was sold last year for $41 billion."

—*The Economist, January 2005*

You can see how AT&T may have developed this myopic point of view. First-generation cellular, or 1G, was defined by bricklike bag phones with bulky car antennas (see Figure 1.3). They were limited to niche professional users, hardcore road warriors, and safety-conscious consumers. When driving in North America, you could travel through vast expanses where the device did not work. At the time, mobile phones were huge and expensive ($1,500 or more), and service also was expensive and not available everywhere.

Figure 1.3   A typical 1G "brick phone"

Key Insight

Like many emerging technologies, wireless looked unattractive and uneconomical at the outset—until consumers understood the true value of mobility.

Second Generation: Wireless Takes Off

Despite the significant barriers to adoption, early analog mobile services still provided significant value to a small segment of high-end users. But it was the introduction of low-cost digital technology and a dominant global standard, Global System for Mobile Communications (GSM), which enabled wireless to become one of the fastest-growing technologies in history. Code Division Multiple Access (CDMA) offered a competing standard to GSM, but it gained very little traction outside the United States due to intellectual property (IP) ownership issues with Qualcomm and other firms. By converting communication signals into 1s and 0s, wireless systems could provide a higher-quality experience with smaller, cheaper handsets. This increased the number of users they could serve in a given coverage area, thus reducing their overall operational costs. Digital also enabled wireless services to easily carry data over the same networks as voice calls, opening a whole new set of potential applications and eventually higher-speed data services (sometimes called 2.5G). By 2003, 2G cellular had driven the total number of wireless users in the world past the total number of fixed-line telephone users (see Figure 1.4), and it never looked back.

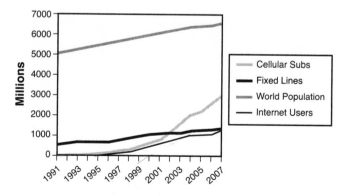

Figure 1.4   Growth in cellular phone usage[5]

WiFi: Making Everyone a Communications Company

As cellular was following its natural and political evolution, a new technology called WiFi was emerging from the edges in the homes of consumers and offices of small businesses. The killer aspect of WiFi was that it used the unlicensed part of the airwaves. This meant that anyone could plug in a WiFi access point and have broadband up and running within 150 feet. The ease of use and elimination of wires made WiFi an instant hit, with over 178,000 hot spots globally as of 2007.[6] When WiFi chipsets became standard in new laptops and many popular destinations incorporated hot spots, WiFi really took off. Now WiFi is even used to carry Internet voice (or voice over IP) for free as an alternative to fixed-line or cellular phone calls. Figure 1.5 shows the incredible growth of WiFi devices.

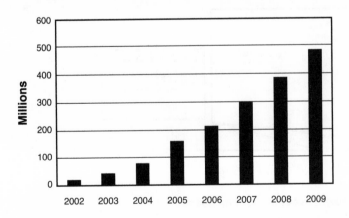

Figure 1.5   Sales of WiFi devices[7]

> **Key Insight**
>
> WiFi disrupted the traditional telecom cost model by using free air-waves and low-cost electronics to give users easy broadband access.

Yet, as with 1G cellular, very few analysts saw the long-term prom-ise of WiFi in its early stages. In fact, what analysts thought was a $200 million market before 2000 quickly became a $2 billion plus market for WiFi-related equipment and services by 2004.[8]

Third Generation: Unfulfilled Promises

2G wireless needed only basic voice and text to ignite a revolution where "mobility" was the killer app. But 3G started with high expecta-tions to deliver a new, unplugged broadband experience that would support a whole new breed of multimedia applications. The dominant theory at the time was that users would pay more for the new, rich set of broadband services that 3G could offer, presenting a large revenue opportunity. In fact, the Strategis Group predicted that 3G-related revenues would reach $33 billion in 2000. The expectations were so high that leading wireless carriers in Europe paid a total of $70 billion for 3G licenses.[9] Unfortunately, this "irrational exuberance" led to over $160 billion in debt and an average drop in stock price of 60% among these same companies. 3G services have been extremely slow to pene-trate the market and deliver real revenues.[10] (Actual revenues were about $5 billion in 2004 using a generous definition of 3G services.[11]) So why did 3G fail to deliver after 2G was so successful? The primary impediments to 3G's success have been the following:

- **Outdated performance targets**—3G was designed to be competitive with broadband speeds in 1998 of about 250 kilo-bits per second (Kbps). These speeds recently have increased dramatically, to well over 1Mbps, but 3G did not.
- **Intellectual property ownership**—Because of the technol-ogy selected for 3G (CDMA), IP and licensing costs became a

significant issue. A few companies (Qualcomm and others) own a significant share of the supporting IP, resulting in royalties of several dollars per handset.

- **WiFi disruption**—Because of its higher speeds and disruptive economics due to free spectrum and cheap devices, WiFi's growth may have undermined the rollout of 3G and its perceived benefits.

- **Lack of compelling applications**—So where is the killer app? Other than faster web access, no other real bandwidth grabbers were being heavily used, because TV and wireless gaming were still relatively small markets.

- **Handset limitations**—Until the iPhone, the basic handset design changed only incrementally as bandwidth started to increase. Browsing the web still required a sluggish translation to have the page content fit the small screen, offsetting many of the improvements in bandwidth.

Key Insight

Wireless providers overinvested in 3G on the promise of wireless broadband revenues, but it has fallen far short of expectations.

4G Wireless: Enabling the Digital Swarm

Despite some of the setbacks, never before has the future of wireless communications been so promising, with nearly 4 billion users worldwide.[12] New technologies and standards looming on the horizon have the potential to create major disruptions not only in the wireless sector, but in communications as a whole. Whereas 3G networks were really about better technology to deliver more of the same, 4G networks are about new technology coupled with a transformation in how people use wireless, moving control to the user. I call this transformation the Digital Swarm. This book explores the underlying forces coming together to shape the Digital Swarm and how they will change the game.

2

Digital Swarm Drivers

"Technology giveth and technology taketh away. No business model, art form, or practice has an inherent right to exist: it has to fit in with the social, technological, and market realities of its day."

—*Paul Miller, Web evangelist*

This chapter discusses the ten social, technological, political, and economic forces that will shape the Digital Swarm over the next decade. These key drivers are shown in Figure 2.1.

This chapter examines each of these drivers in more detail, starting with the largest potential disruptors. Key questions are posed for how they may shape the Digital Swarm in the future. Rather than attempt to answer these key questions now or predict their outcome, we will use them to stimulate the development of future scenarios in the next chapter.

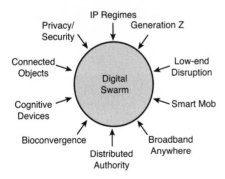

Figure 2.1   Key drivers of the Digital Swarm

Smart Mob: Empowered Groups with Greater Impact

In Stephen King's book *Cell*, a cell-phone-based attack is used to take over the minds of large populations and turn them into zombies. In the Philippines, cell phones have been used to overthrow governments. In the United States, cell phones have driven grassroot support in presidential campaigns (Howard Dean, Barrack Obama). Several experiments have shown that wireless can be an accelerator in the spread of social networks.[1]

Social networks thrive because their users subscribe to unwritten rules that protect the common good. Violators of these rules are policed and sometimes shunned by network participants. The notion that people act in a way that preserves the common good, sometimes investing time, effort, and even money without expecting immediate payback, is called the "gift economy." This term was coined by Howard Rheingold after he studied different groups of users interacting with wireless technology and each other in trend-setting markets like Japan and Helsinki. In wireless networks, this gift economy rises to a completely new level, where users are willing to offer services and information about themselves to benefit the population of other mobile users. Powerful new applications such as intelligent highways, people tracking, security threat detection, and even human computing will only succeed based on a high level of cooperation among users.

Key Insight

Will wireless fundamentally change human and organizational behavior? If so, will it have a positive or negative net impact on communities and organizations?

Privacy and Security: Big Brother Inside

Whether it's a group of mischievous MIT students downloading Paris Hilton's address book from her phone at the Grammys, or hackers rewriting code in the iPhone, wireless security has been escalating as a pivotal issue for the future unwired world. The spread of viruses in wireless devices follows an almost biological pattern, in which devices within close proximity are more likely to pass on a virus, like humans passing on a cold. The wireless devices of the future will be able to access almost any network in the background without the subscriber's knowledge, thus creating many opportunities for moving malicious code from one device to another.

Wireless privacy is as important as, if not more important than, wireless security. With the advent of GPS and location information accurate to less than 1 meter linked to other user activities, the amount of data related to a given user's behavior throughout the day has exploded. Because they are always on, mobile devices produce a persistent record of where users are. The analysis of this data is called "reality mining," and it can produce a much more accurate account of someone's whereabouts than his or her own.[2] Insurance carriers have begun offering discounts for drivers willing to have their driving habits tracked via wireless GPS information. Casinos track the movement of chips across the gaming floor and can infer the betting behaviors of different players based on this information. Schools have begun tracking the movement of students, and government agencies are tracking employees' movements using wireless tags. The possibilities are endless. But who will control all this data in the future?

Key Insight

Which way will the privacy/security scale tip for wireless? Closed versus open? Fear versus trust? How will society and governments respond?

Seamless Mobility: Blurring Geographic and Work-Life Boundaries

As devices get smarter and users can access resources and applications from anywhere, the domains of work, home, and personal life will eventually become blurred. Will it really matter when, where, and how you watch your ethics training video, as long as you do it? Will anyone be willing to carry more than one device that supports the full spectrum of enterprise and entertainment applications?

We are already seeing strong signals today as users are insisting on bringing their consumer-based applications and devices into their work environment. Although CIOs have initially resisted this push due to concerns about security and support costs, this shift seems inevitable. The major online brands, network operators, device manufacturers, and even retailers are all gradually pushing into the enterprise with crossover offerings. As wireless devices become the remote control for our lives, it will be much harder for users to separate work and life applications. This places an enormous responsibility on the enterprise to "go with the flow." It must come up with ways to manage this radically changing ecosystem of individually selected and controlled devices. It may require loose guidelines for proper behavior.

In some cases, users can actually create their own wireless networks beyond the home. Mesh networks (such as Fon in the U.K.) use the power of peer-to-peer communications to allow users to connect directly with each other and also act as "nodes" in the network. In many ways, the users *are* the network. This is much like peer-to-peer networks for file sharing, such as Kazaa and eDonkey, where users operate without a central management authority based on open standards. This lack of central infrastructure makes the economics of mesh networks very attractive. The bulk of the costs are the devices, not the infrastructure, as with cellular networks.

Key Insight

What will be the balance of control between employers and employees over wireless devices and applications as the home and work environments converge? And who will bear the cost?

Cognitive Devices: Contextual Intelligence and Decision-Making

Back in the 1980s, artificial intelligence (AI) became taboo, with glorious promises and fantastic failures like intelligent cars and personal robots. In this first wave, AI failed on two fronts: The technology wasn't ready for prime time, and people weren't ready for the social implications of relinquishing important decisions to a machine.

Fast-forward two decades, and a resurgence in AI is occurring, hidden from the average customer, but very much a part of our lives and how we make decisions. Whether it's learning algorithms updating our preferences on Amazon or TiVo, surveillance cameras interpreting video and knowing when someone is shoplifting, or the iPhone determining whether we want to talk or text based on the phone's orientation, context-based decisions are embedded in many things around us. Today's wireless devices are fairly limited in their understanding of the individual user and their ability to switch among available networks (such as WiFi and 3G). But as additional computing power becomes available to mobile devices, more intelligent or "cognitive" functions are emerging. These include knowing what frequencies and networks are available for use, knowing where the user is and what services are available, and knowing the user's situation and preferences to tailor communications and applications accordingly. For instance, knowing that a user is running (based on her vital signs) versus relaxing may drastically change the types of applications she wants to access.

Billions have already been spent on deploying software-defined radios for military applications. It is just a matter of time until commercial versions are available that can access almost any network and adapt to each user's unique situation. For this reason, cognitive devices are the biggest "game-changer" among 4G technologies, because they shift the power in wireless networks to the user.

Key Insight

How will all of these smart, context-aware users interact? Who will manage and police the overall system to ensure fair allocations of resources to everyone?

The Power of Embedded Objects: Processors and Connectivity in Everything

Already, machine-to-machine (M2M) communications far outstrip human-to-human communications. It's just invisible to us. In 2007, 10 billion microprocessors were sold, many of them embedded in things that communicate, such as cell phones, home controls, and toys.[3] Some projections have the number of connected objects reaching 100 billion in the next decade! This distributed processing is enabling sensor networks to be designed for very powerful applications, such as remote equipment monitoring, threat detection (fires, floods, terrorism), and the coordination of assets (ships, aircraft, cars).

Wembley Stadium uses mousetraps with sensors and microprocessors to report back to a monitoring terminal. This keeps a worker from having to check each trap. Appliances such as coffee makers and refrigerators can relay information and can be controlled via remote communications and processing. (We will no longer have to check if the beer is cold!) In the defense sector, unmanned aerial vehicles (UAVs) can quickly form networks and make decisions in real time, reducing the time between sensing and killing the target from hours to a matter of minutes or even seconds.

Key Insight

How will the global grid of connected objects and sensors change how we do business and lead our lives? Will we sacrifice privacy to make better decisions with better information?

Generation Z (Echo Boomers): Spreading Their Mobility DNA

"14-year-old girls will become the TIOs (Teenage Information Officers) of every household."

—*Taki Papudopoulis, President of Drexel University*

Unlike the mainstream views on privacy and security, younger generations (Gen Z) have turned this threat into an opportunity to open up their lives and be completely networked all the time. It is clear that teens and young adults view technology as an extension of their lives and personalities, versus a tool or necessity to communicate, like most adults do. Ask someone under 20 if he has a landline phone or an email account, and he will look at you like your head is on backward. In fact, it is expected that 26 million American adults will not own a landline phone by 2012.[4] That is because they have grown up with and honed a different set of communications skills using an integrated mix of text, instant messaging (IM), and shared media. This allows them to communicate many more streams of information than earlier generations. In addition, they are extremely comfortable with transparency of their personal lives, as evidenced by the significant popularity of social networking sites such as Facebook and MySpace. Their need to stay networked is constant. Services like Helio's Buddy Beacon and Dodgeball offer real-time opportunities to track the location of other individuals in your network or even soon-to-be network.

Key Insight

Will Gen Z end up conforming to more conservative views of organizations and networks as they mature? Or will they drive radically new models for how wireless is used in business and personal life?

Bioconvergence: Wireless and Human Health

Already, wireless technology is changing how healthcare is delivered. Services like Healthpia and Myca offer the ability to monitor patient health indicators via mobile phones and even to connect to a doctor via a mobile videoconference. Mobile devices in the future may include not only these features but also biosensors for detecting potentially harmful contaminants or pathogens in the user's environment.

Just as cell phones are becoming mobile wallets, they may also become mobile medical records for patients. A number of countries, such as France, have mandated electronic ID cards that include critical medical information for each individual. If someone in a remote area needs immediate medical care, her integrated health records could be made available via her smartphone to facilitate faster care, potentially saving her life. This brings us back to the privacy debate, because more sensitive information is accessible via your wireless devices. The same question exists: Is the benefit worth the risk?

Cell phones may not only change the delivery of healthcare; they may also affect the study of medicine and the development of new cures. While biology can be used to understand the spread of mobile viruses, the reverse is also true. The Centers for Disease Control and Prevention (CDC) recently used the virtual game World of Warcraft to understand the potential spread and effects of a pandemic.[5] Tracking how new applications, or even malicious code, spread through a mobile population could also provide insight into how a pandemic may spread across a population of people.

Key Insight

Will wireless become a differentiator and game-changer in health-care and the prevention and treatment of disease, or just another communications tool?

The Vanishing Company

As employees become more capable of performing business functions outside the traditional corporate boundaries, the organizational hierarchy is becoming challenged in most companies. In the late 1990s and early 2000s, telecommuting allowed employees to perform basic functions in their homes via fairly controlled access to the company's private network. As the web became more accepted as an enterprise platform and more business applications became "e-enabled," the percentage of functions employees could do remotely grew. In some cases, large companies have created virtual workforces like JetBlue's Call Center and the Infosys Consulting Team. Linux proved that large-scale product development projects could be executed without a true organizational hierarchy. Future wireless technology will further flatten the organizational structure by putting the power of the enterprise in people's hands and allowing them to operate and make informed decisions from anywhere.

With the computing and storage power that will be available on future devices, there will be no need to be in the office, other than for collaboration and social interaction. The boundaries between work and home will essentially vanish as people will choose when and how they work.[6] The implications are that employees will have an enormous influence on which technologies and applications the company uses, preferring the ones they find most convenient in their own lives. In addition, companies will struggle to maintain an identity and culture as employees act more as talented individuals than as part of an integrated workforce.

Key Insight

How will the Digital Swarm affect the structure of organizations? Will they become highly decentralized or centralized but with greater mobility?

Low-End Disruption: Innovations from Emerging Markets

In his book *The Fortune at the Bottom of the Pyramid*, C. K. Prahalad examines the tremendous potential for market disruptions from products and services that address the needs of the poorest 2.7 billion people in the world.[7] Wireless operators that serve this low-end market, such as Millicom and MTN, are some of the fastest-growing and most profitable service providers in the world. As you can probably imagine, wireless penetration in less economically developed regions is much higher than fixed-line phones in those same regions, creating a "leapfrog" effect.[8]

Here are some recent examples of wireless-enabled products and services targeting the bottom of the pyramid:

- **eChoupal**—Farmers and fishermen in India can check market prices via mobile devices before making the long trek to take their goods to market, more efficiently matching supply and demand.

- **Microfinance**—Small loans (less than $100) are provided to individuals in remote villages through a network of banks and communities connected via wireless phones.

- **Virtual doctors**—Doctors and healthcare workers can support basic medical services for many patients in remote locations via wireless video and data links. This keeps the doctors and healthcare workers from having to make time-consuming and sometimes dangerous journeys to see the patients.

As Clay Christiansen illustrates in *The Innovator's Dilemma*, product disruption typically comes from the noncustomers of today.[9]

Many of the traditional wireless service providers ignore the low-income customer segments. However, the sheer number of subscribers in this segment makes them a powerful group with enormous potential to shape the Digital Swarm.

Key Insight

Will wireless solutions addressing the low end of the market evolve to disrupt the high end, or will we end up with a wireless divide between the haves and the have-nots?

IP Regimes and the Wireless Ecosystem: Shifting Control and Profit Motives

History has proven that standards can be an enormous catalyst for the growth of a given product category. UNIX, TCP/IP, and GSM have all shown the power of open global standards. Many closed standards have also generated value for markets and intellectual property (IP) owners such as iTunes, Windows, BlackBerry Server, and Blu-ray. As mentioned in the preceding chapter, CDMA was limited by requiring significant royalties on each handset, versus opening up the standard fully. As a result, GSM quickly dominated the world, covering over two thirds of the world's subscribers versus less than one fourth for CDMA.

More recently, the Chinese developed their own 3G standard because they did not want to pay royalties on each CDMA handset to Qualcomm and other companies that owned the IP. Given that China has the most wireless subscribers in the world, they have the market muscle to make this type of decision. With a new set of players entering the wireless ecosystem with different IP strategies, it is unclear whether standards will harmonize or fracture and whether governments, vendors, or even users will determine the outcome.

Key Insight

Who will control the IP that will enable 4G wireless and the Digital Swarm? Will it rely on open or closed standards?

Frameworks for Understanding the Future

The drivers presented in this chapter will not act in isolation in the unwired future. Instead, they will act together as a complex web of persistent trends and unpredictable shocks to shape the future. Systems Thinking is a useful framework to apply to an environment such as this, where significant complexity and uncertainty exist.[10] Systems Thinking lays out all the major variables and indicates both the interrelationships and causal pathways among variables. Sometimes these relationships are counterintuitive and are more easily revealed after the model is developed and visualized.

Let's apply a Systems approach to the forces impacting the future of the Digital Swarm. We start by taking into account all the major drivers discussed and creating new variables where needed to explain some of the interrelationships in the system, as shown in Figure 2.2. In the diagram, directional arrows show cause and effect, and plus and minus signs along each path indicate a positive or negative relationship.

From this model, we can see that many things can impact the growth of wireless and primary drivers, such as killer applications and network trust. For example, concern about the health or environmental impact of cell phones could limit the interest in integrating wireless with clothing and the body. In turn, this could limit embedded sensors and the ability of cognitive devices to make contextual decisions. This may also limit seamless mobility, because user devices would not be adaptive enough to work across all network types. Consequently, killer applications could be stifled. Systems diagrams like this are also very useful for helping us contemplate what future scenarios may be plausible by examining the key variables and their interrelationships.

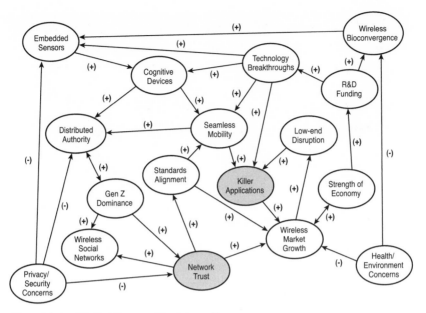

Figure 2.2   Digital Swarm Systems diagram

Key Insight

The Digital Swarm future will be driven by a large number of interrelated but unpredictable factors. Systems thinking can be used as a tool to make sense of these complex interactions.

The next chapter develops in detail two future scenarios for the unwired world. The outlines of these two scenarios are derived from the Digital Swarm Systems model discussed in this chapter.

Scenario Planning as a Strategic Planning Tool

Scenario planning has been used for several decades to help organizations better prepare for an uncertain future. Shell has used scenario planning extensively to understand where the future environment may be headed so as to inform better investment decisions for its business.

The objective of scenario planning is to sketch out strategically different futures for an industry or market that could impact your organization's future success. The focus is on external forces beyond your control.[11]

Here are the basic steps in scenario planning:

1. **Identify important forces shaping the future,** including economic, social, political, technological, legal, and other forces. Explore what relationships exist among these forces to determine if they are mutually compatible. Go beyond the symptoms to identify the fundamental drivers of future change.

2. **Distinguish between trends and uncertainties.** Long-term trends are forces you are willing to "bet your strategy" on. Uncertainties are forces that are more unpredictable in the time horizon of interest. For each uncertainty, identify outcomes that bound the range of possibilities. Explore the deeper interrelationships among the key uncertainties by developing influence diagrams such as the one shown in Figure 2.2.

3. **Develop multiple scenarios** by varying the outcomes of the uncertainties that have the highest impact. Then incorporate the highest-impact trends to get to coherent, plausible alternative futures. Finally, develop the scenarios in narrative form, including drivers, key issues, and signposts.

Scenario planning does not provide "answers"; instead, it offers insights into where the future may go. It is about being "roughly right" versus "precisely wrong" when the future environment is uncertain and complex, as is the case for the future wireless market and emerging Digital Swarm.

Some variables are highly uncertain and could play out across a wide range of outcomes (like network trust and killer applications). Other variables may have similar direction and intensity in all scenarios, indicating trends (like technology breakthroughs and distributed authority). The unpredictable variables require flexible strategies that can respond to a range of outcomes, as shown in Table 2.1.

TABLE 2.1   Unpredictable Variables

Variable	Flexible Strategy Challenge for the Organization
Network trust	Mission-critical versus casual wireless applications
Wireless market growth	Limited choices versus highly dynamic wireless options
Strength of the econ-omy	Abundant versus limited funding for wireless initiatives
Killer applications	Rapid adoption of new apps versus an incremental approach
Standards alignment	Tied to one wireless standard or access to many standards
Gen Z dominance	Adopt Gen Z behaviors broadly or suppress them
Privacy and security	Open versus closed wireless security policy and systems
Health and environ-ment	Emphasis on wireless safety and disposal versus none

Other variables are more pervasive in all possible future scenarios, as shown in Table 2.2. While some of these vary slightly across scenarios, they can generally be considered trends that you can "bet your strategy" on or respond to in any future, because they have enormous momentum for the next decade.

TABLE 2.2   Variables That Indicate Trends

Trend	Organization's Response Challenge
Technology	Rapid adoption of new wireless technology into operations
Low-end disruption	Scouting and leveraging low-end wireless applications
Wireless social networks	Wireless access to internal and external social networks
Embedded sensors	Integrate wireless sensors into products and operations
Distributed authority	Flat organization model with decision authority at the edge
Seamless mobility	Wireless applications that leverage "everywhere" coverage
Cognitive devices	Large investment in devices with highly flexible capability

These trends will interact differently with uncertain variables to create the two different future scenarios described in the next chapter. Both the variables and the trends create unique challenges for any organization trying to develop a wireless strategy for the future. We will discuss some of these challenges and potential success strategies later in the book.

3

Possible Future Scenarios: Convergence, Collision, Confluence

"Predicting the future of the mobile market is like going to PetSmart and trying to select a goldfish that won't die in the 20 min[utes] it takes you to drive it home and put it in a fish bowl."

—*Chris Wilson, "Planting in the Mobile Market"*

This chapter presents two possible scenarios for the unwired future, developed from the drivers and themes identified in the first two chapters. Scenario planning is a powerful tool for exploring the range of alternative futures for the Digital Swarm. It helps leaders challenge existing assumptions and inform critical decisions. These scenarios represent potential boundaries or extremes for the unwired future over the next decade. Although it is highly unlikely that either of these scenarios will happen in its entirety, it is highly likely that a combination of elements from both scenarios will exist in what actually takes place. By developing flexible strategies that pay off at the extremes, you can position your organization for success across a range of possible futures instead of anchoring your strategy to a "point forecast" for a highly uncertain environment.

The first scenario (Scenario A) is Nature Aligns, in which a wholesale transformation occurs in the wireless ecosystem. Humans are nodes in a vast and rich network, and enormous opportunities exist for value creation around new applications. The second scenario (Scenario B) is Killer Bees, in which the world fractures along technology and standards. Economic boundaries and wireless networks, devices, and applications present as many threats, such as global wireless epidemics, as opportunities to business and society as a whole. The alternative futures depicted by these scenarios are meant to represent outer boundaries for challenging business strategies; they are not meant to predict the future. Figure 3.1 shows technology disruption as a persistent force over time and social trust in networks as the major unknown tipping us toward one of these possible futures. While obviously many other possible scenarios could be developed, these two were chosen as reasonable bounds on where the future may go. We can use them as a basis for challenging current assumptions and developing forward-looking strategies.

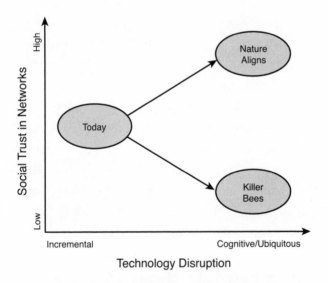

Figure 3.1   Interaction of major Digital Swarm drivers

Scenario A: Nature Aligns

"When you piece together these different technological, economic, and social components, the result is an infrastructure that makes certain kinds of human actions possible that were never possible before."

—*Howard Rheingold, Smart Mobs*

In this future, advances in wireless are creating enormous value all around us, with innovations led by mobile virtual network operators (MVNOs), device manufacturers, and artificial intelligence software vendors. Self-organizing networks with end-to-end quality of service (QoS) are the norm. The digital divide has been effectively erased as broadband wireless is a universal right in developed areas, much like other utilities. Public WiFi has become an important social program for economic development. It has been coupled with the $100 computer and $20 smartphone to drive significant economic development in the Third World. Wireless provides other social benefits beyond just voice and data, including disease and disaster tracking, weather prediction, and security/terror early-warning systems. Body-area networks (BANs), where technology is integrated with a user's clothing or is implanted in their body, monitor vital signs and distribute drugs within the body. The wireless immersion experience is widely available to those who want it, causing large organizations to flatten further. The "gift economy" dominates as users behave in a way that contributes to the common good. Those who fail to conform to the unwritten rules are policed by the masses. The "wisdom of crowds" is viewed as more powerful than any individual wireless user.

The following sections describe the outcomes of each of the key variables in the Nature Aligns scenario.

Network Trust

In this world, defenses stay well ahead of threats for wireless cyber-security. More importantly, users self-police the environment for potentially threatening behavior, much like the volunteers patrolling the Internet for al-Qaeda activity or the Neighborhood Watch concept today. As a result, typical users feel very comfortable sharing detailed profile information, including financial and medical records, via wireless networks. Although occasional incidents occur in which mobile phones are compromised, they are localized and quickly remedied via technology and policy upgrades, which are automatically updated via software in the user's mobile device. User location information is leveraged by all industries to enhance the benefit delivered to consumers. Companies understand the need to protect this information, and they take appropriate measures to do so. Users can jump onto virtually any network, from peer-to-peer networks and wireless local area networks (LANs), to advanced mobile networks, via their smart devices. They feel comfortable that universal security standards and built-in protection on their devices will ensure secure communications and transactions. Overall trust in wireless networks is extremely high.

Technology Breakthroughs

Technology has continued to advance at a torrid pace across all parts of the wireless value chain, including networks, devices, and applications. In particular, advances in the human interface have enabled the mobile device to provide a rich, immersive multimedia experience. Retinal projection (projecting a much larger, high-definition display in space), coupled with flawless speech processing, has virtually eliminated the need for clunky keystrokes and has increased the amount of "bandwidth to the brain." Devices have taken on a full range of cognitive capabilities:

- Sensing the user's environment and situation, including weather, movement, location, biometrics, and activities
- Finding and accessing available network resources, including available frequencies, bandwidth, and applications via network crawlers and smart agents
- Making decisions about where, how, and when the user will want to access different applications, depending on her situation or "presence"

These devices are widely available to all types of users at reasonable price points. Differences are driven primarily by style choices. Successful device manufacturers lead the pack in transforming the user interface and also manage to integrate value-added services with the handset to give the user full decision support. In some cases, these intelligent devices begin to push into the realm of "singularity," where machines achieve cognitive capabilities equivalent to those of humans.[1] In Nature Aligns, these developments are all viewed as positive steps toward a more fulfilling life for mobile netizens.

Wireless broadband has become highly reliable and ubiquitous as standards have driven toward complete interoperability among LANs and wide area networks (WANs) of all types. This includes mesh networks, where users themselves become nodes within the network to relay communications via the most efficient route. This forces network providers to choose between a low-cost volume model and moving into subscription and pay-per-use applications. Some networks become dedicated to machine-to-machine communications, such as sensor networks, and others service both users and stand-alone devices.

Wireless Market Growth

The wireless market has experienced steady growth over the last decade, reaching 6 billion users out of a world population of 9 billion. A significant part of this growth comes from the developing world, where wireless has bypassed traditional wireline networks as the primary communications medium. Even in the United States and Europe, where wireline networks have deep roots, 30% of the population relies solely on wireless for their everyday communications. Area codes and local telephone exchanges have become artifacts in old directories, because your mobile number follows you wherever you are. While voice calls are now free anywhere in the world, because they are indistinguishable from data streams, data has taken on many different levels of service and associated pricing. Even though broadband wireless is ubiquitous, network operators can tailor the QoS to optimize the performance of specific applications, and users are willing to pay a premium for this. For instance, multiplayer gaming has become highly immersive, with visual and sensory interactions requiring significant bandwidth with very low delay and low variability. Serious gamers pay for a special service upgrade that kicks in when the network identifies them as connecting to a multiplayer game. So while revenue growth is limited for traditional network operators, they can find profitable segments that value unique levels of service. Other operators in this future, such as Skype, are strictly volume-driven. These operators are looking to accumulate users and earn revenue via advertising, selling user profile statistics, and concierge-type services. Very few operators exist on a vertical proprietary content model (once tried by Disney and ESPN), because the large content and application players, such as Murdoch and Sony, choose to play the field through all wireless networks.

Strength of Economy

The global economy has continued to expand at a steady pace. Universal access to wireless networks has closed the wealth gap between developed and developing nations and has brought transparency to global trade. The result is a true free market around the world as strong-armed politics are trumped by the power of the masses and what is deemed best for society. The tracking of goods around the world has become pervasive, resulting in a more distributed global commerce system. Traditional ports and hubs are no longer critical, because suppliers and buyers can easily connect in an open marketplace and find the easiest and cheapest route to transact. Brick-and-mortar retailers have become nothing more than demo centers for consumers to touch and feel products before purchasing them. Likewise, power has shifted from the traditional financial markets, because information transparency has virtually eliminated the advantage of large banks and brokerage houses. Exchanges like NYSE and LSE have become vehicles to consolidate and reconcile information, but they are no longer needed to value a given stock, because this happens through a broad, global market. Wall Street is a shadow of its glory days in the '80s and '90s. The average investor or trader has the same access to tools and information as large institutions.

As a result, average investment returns and savings are up. New hedge funds emerge every day, because smart individuals can promote their track records and profiles easily to large groups of people who can invest. Peer-to-peer lending has finally passed traditional bank lending as the primary vehicle for personal and auto loans, and it is making strides into the mortgage market. Small players and market aggregators are running the show, with wireless as a key enabler.

Killer Applications

An explosion in innovative, compelling wireless applications on both the business and consumer sides has helped fuel the continued investment in universal network coverage. Killer apps are targeted at all customer segments, including those in the lower economic strata, where it is more about simplicity, volume, and efficiency. The following wireless applications are seeing the biggest breakthroughs in user adoption:

- **Interactive multiplayer gaming**—Everything from virtual casinos to incredibly realistic adventure games and sports, including physically engaging the user (started by the Wii over a decade ago!).

- **Video entertainment**—The ability to download, watch, and exchange high-definition video entertainment, from short clips to full-length movies in real time, projected in multiple formats by mobile devices. Blockbuster and Netflix are long gone.

- **Concierge services**—Recommendations on everything from dining, flowers, and local hot spots to critical services like traffic routing, repairs, and medical facilities.

- **Decision support**—Using real-time updating and access to critical information to drive better decisions for individuals and groups based on the user's location and context, whether it's coaches on a field, regional sales teams, or soldiers on a battlefield.

- **Immersive touring**—Allowing users to experience the activity or trip before they jump into it and commit. This is more than on-screen tours. It also includes virtual-reality extensions (gloves, glasses, olfactory stimulators) networked via a mobile device.

- **Interactive education and training**—Educators can harness the power of pervasive mobile broadband to deliver a balance of human- and machine-delivered learning, extending the traditional boundaries of the classroom.

- **Virtual healthcare**—From patients on vacation being monitored and diagnosed remotely by their primary care physician or specialist, to emergency response care for seniors or patients in distress, new applications have made healthcare omnipresent.

- **Remote sensing, monitoring, and control**—Cell phones have truly become the "remote control for your life" through a combination of distributed sensors and applications that can manage key metrics such as energy and water usage, carbon emissions, security, and care of the elderly, children, and pets.

- **Polling and prediction markets**—Wireless users can quickly assess popular or expert-group opinions on key questions about a range of topics, including products, markets, and politics.

- **Distributed supply chain**—Product tracking, routing, and security across the supply chain to allow optimization, adaptation, and self-healing based on new conditions or failures.

- **Personal security**—Detecting threats around mobile individuals and facilities or homes by integrating local sensor information, threat databases, and individual context.

- **Content management from multiple devices and sources**—Applications that allow you to easily transfer, synchronize, and manage content across many platforms, including fixed and mobile devices and peripherals, like cameras, MP3 players, and automobiles, anytime and anywhere. This includes automatic updating and refresh of content based on personal preference via the most appropriate network resource.

- **Smart shopping**—Gives consumers the power to research, compare, and decide in real time based on current product or service information, wherever they are.

- **Emergency services coordination**—Allows first responders such as fire, police, and paramedic units to coordinate actions based on real-time situation updating, including location, video, audio, and environmental sensing.

These applications straddle the consumer and enterprise sectors, with no real distinction or boundaries between work and life applications. Benefit is measured in terms of improving the overall quality of the work-life continuum in terms of impact and efficiency. Whether it's maximizing the entertainment value of limited free time, being able to watch a training video while waiting at an airport, or being able to quickly tap into a prediction market to assess the potential of a new business plan, the onslaught of killer apps in this future has dramatically changed how wireless integrates with our business and personal lives.

Standards Alignment

Just like the early growth of GSM, the wireless world has figured out the power of standards. Key standards bodies such as IEEE, ETSI, ITU, and others have come together to align the overall standards road map to ensure a seamless wireless experience anywhere on the planet. Political and competitive issues that have been impediments to past standards are easily handled through a more effective ITU governing process involving wireless leaders and sample representation from all markets. Companies that do not play by the rules are not allowed in the bigger game. It is now possible to take one device and connect to any network (including directly with other users) within range, use applications of interest, and resolve the appropriate security, billing, and user management updates for each user activity. Standard interfaces and protocols allow devices and networks to negotiate behind the scenes to determine the right network resources and quality of service and then actively manage this, no matter who the network owner is. This results in high trust in network performance and security, as discussed earlier.

Low-End Disruption

As mentioned in the preceding chapter, the divide between the haves and the have-nots in the world has closed significantly. This includes economic status, access to resources, and communications capability. Much of this tremendous progress in the developing world comes from technology-enabled leapfrog solutions that deliver equivalent or more value at a dramatically lower cost. In fact, many of the killer apps mentioned earlier come from developing markets like India, China, and Brazil. They are driven by the necessity to solve real socioeconomic problems such as education, healthcare, and market access for large populations that previously lived on less than $2 per day.

Wireless Social Networks

With the transparency of continuous peer-to-peer communications across boundaries, individuals and groups have become more powerful than the companies and governments they associate with. Most individuals belong to 30 or more social networks covering a range of personal and professional interests. Social networking sites take on continuous access and location awareness as they become dominated by wireless users. Some large players fail to take advantage of this new dimension in providing useful services and instead use it only to sell more targeted advertising. These large players slip in numbers as new upstarts manage to gain large user bases by focusing on specific interest areas. Many more self-organizing platforms like Ning use Web 3.0 open contextual web platforms to steal the low end of this sector. Advertising revenues are on the rise for networks that have maintained the user's trust, and they constantly innovate to deliver new tools and services accessible via wireless devices.

Seamless Mobility

As we have seen throughout the history of emerging technologies, when standards align, exceptional market growth tends to occur. This is the case in Nature Aligns. The invisible boundaries created by carriers and regulators no longer exist to stop users from having access to all available networks at a given location and devices that can communicate and process applications with these networks. Given that users can get similar coverage and performance at almost any location around the globe, the advantages of specific cities and economic centers have begun to erode. Where people choose to work or live is more about the continued need for live interaction versus access to resources. Most network operators offer a continuum from WANs, spanning hundreds or even thousands of miles, down to pico-cells or personal-area networks (PANs), spanning a few meters. The cascade of networks within a given operator and across operators is seamlessly interconnected based on the universal standards discussed earlier. Handoffs are seamless and invisible to the user, and account-ing and security are managed via open, interconnected databases across providers.

Embedded Sensors

Sensors have become embedded everywhere—clothing, homes, autos, gardens, offices, classrooms, factories, shopping malls, and even golf courses. There is no place that does not have some form of sensor, whether it is simply environmental (temperature, vibra-tions, pressure) or more a complex monitoring of activities and behaviors. People readily accept millions of eyes watching them as a trade-off for better information access, efficiency, and security. Peo-ple also have a higher level of trust in wireless networks. The con-cept of humans as sensors, previously relegated to military applications, has become mainstream. Sensors are embedded in devices people carry and are even implanted in the body, net-worked to form BANs.

Gen Z Dominance

Generation Z, defined as those born after 1990,[2] has become the catalyst for many of the changes in the wireless arena. Having grown up with a cell phone in their hand, they view mobile devices as an extension of their physical and mental being. Everything in their lives—from education, family communications, and time management, to planning their social activities and managing their entertainment experience—is done with a mobile phone at the center. Most dates are organized via cell phones—sometimes even on-the-fly the night of the event by knowing the profiles and locations of the parties involved. Wireless social networking is *the* medium that Gen Z'ers communicate with. They do not own landline phones, nor do they have email accounts. This creates huge issues for the companies that hire them. But their informed ability to network, create, and decide is a precious commodity every organization wants, so they deal with the nonconformity, including the demands to use the devices and applications of their choice. Gen Z'ers are now in positions of authority and are no longer viewed as radicals, but decision-makers.

Distributed Authority

The Gen Z'ers are not the only ones pushing the boundaries of traditional social and organizational rules. Every consumer and employee who has been empowered with pervasive, cognitive wireless capability is now an organization of one. All the benefits once attributed to being part of a large organization have disappeared. Individuals can access and marshal resources on a global scale more quickly and effectively than big organizations through powerful mobile social networks. As demonstrated by recent government and company takeovers coordinated through ad hoc wireless social networks, or "smart mobs,"[3] authority has truly been atomized. This forces companies, nongovernment organizations (NGOs), and even governments to rethink their value proposition and long-term relevance. Companies that adapt become focused on brand equity, commerce standards, managing the user experience, and open innovation. They become hubs that govern transactions and information exchange among various players in the value chain, and they ensure quality of service and the user experience. Brands that do this well earn a premium and amass significant user and product information that drives their company value. Those that don't, become relics of yesterday's marketplace, where strong players controlled the flow of goods and services and the resulting profits.

Cognitive Devices

Handsets and other wireless devices have taken on lives of their own as they sense the user environment and situation, access resources and information as needed, make and aid decisions, and entertain the user. Top device manufacturers have become world leaders in human factor design, with constantly evolving user interfaces and approaches to maximize "bandwidth to the brain." In fact, brain-machine interfaces (BMIs) come standard with most phones and can take the form of headsets or small probes. Handsets are customized and built to each user using a virtual "fitting" kiosk at wireless stores. Ergonomics are perfectly matched to each user (ear, face, mouth, and eye proportions) and how he wants to wear his personal wireless communicator (clothing-based, implant, handheld, mounted). Almost all devices are equipped with open software platforms that manage the resources and applications the user needs. Downloads, upgrades, one-time applications, scouting software agents, security status, radio frequency allocation, protocols, and standards are all managed via the phone's core software and powerful central processing unit (CPU). Components for the transmission and receipt of wireless signals occur in many frequency bands and support many different types of wireless standards. A decade ago, this technology could only be produced in the lab at a very high per-unit cost. Now, the Moore's Law equivalent for radio components has driven these parts to a minimal cost comparable to most microchips.

Privacy/Security Concerns

Security and privacy breaches are limited to small-scale attacks on individuals. Proliferation of these attacks to larger populations is thwarted by strong security standards, advanced encryption techniques, and user community vigilance in monitoring potential threats. User devices are updated automatically, with the latest protection software and patches based on real-time assessment of threats. Software agents continuously roam networks to test for anomalous behavior or evidence of tampering. Most governments have implemented wireless cyber-security branches, with heavy authority to prosecute violators of network policies. This includes not only information security issues but also misuse of wireless airwaves or "spectrum" outside of standard rules and policies. In fact, very little spectrum is owned privately anymore. Distributed sensors and feedback from operator network access points can quickly determine if any individual user is accessing frequencies already in use or interfering with other users by operating at too high a power level. A wireless "Bill of Rights" has been put in place to protect user information from being abused by companies and other individuals. Retailers, financial institutions, healthcare providers, educational institutions, and wireless network operators are held to the highest standards given the amount of information they control. The last major privacy breach is now five years in the past, and the bank it happened to is no longer in business.

Health and Environmental Concerns

Companies that participate in the wireless ecosystem are held to the same intense standards for protecting the environment and sustainability as other leading companies around the globe. With countries and their citizens holding companies to a higher standard, a new wave of responsible products and services has evolved. Wearable chipsets distribute the radiation from wireless devices to safe levels. Rechargeable fuel cells (methane and hydrogen) eliminate the toxic waste of traditional lithium ion and nickel hydride batteries. Mesh networks utilize existing structures and even user devices for access and relay points versus unsightly cell phone towers.

A Consumer Day in the Life

Heather Manning heard a chirp, indicating that someone was calling her on her wireless device. The chirp was audible only to her, coming through the ear implant connected to her core cognitive radio device, a slim card in her pocket. Since she had given up her fixed-line phone many years back, she did not have to worry about how people would reach her, especially now that broadband was available anywhere she could conceivably go. Her friend, Annie, was calling to find out if she and her son, Jack, wanted to go see the local pro basketball team, the SkyWalkers. Heather did not need to ask Jack, because he loved basketball. In fact, when she pinged Jack's device, it had already decided that the game fit Jack's schedule and personal preferences and responded with a "yes."

Before Annie and her son, Bryan, picked up Heather and Jack, Jack and Bryan had already connected via their smart agents. They found several common social networks they were both in, exchanged their favorite players and dance girls on the SkyWalkers and chatted about tonight's game. Annie had already plotted their route and alternatives by checking real-time traffic updates and had set the entertainment system in the backseat to accept downloads from Bryan's profile for the ride into town. When they arrived at the arena, they each received personalized messages on their devices, indicating areas of interest and special vendor deals and locations. After they were in their seats, the experience came alive as their devices instantly networked into the picocells in their individual seats with real-time replays, stats, product information, and related NBA multimedia clips available via their devices, on demand. With their ear implants, it was easy to hear both the crowd and their personalized audio feeds when desired.

Bryan and Jack could not stop talking about the game on the way home. They sent video feeds of the arena and highlights from the game to select friends and posted them to their profiles. Heather did a quick videocon with her ex-husband, letting him know about the game and that she would drop off Jack at his house on Monday. He reminded her that Jack should sync his latest preferences with the house to make sure his adaptive home environment would be exactly the way Jack likes it (entertainment, climate, lighting, computing). Annie, a diabetic, was checking her blood glucose level trend through the car's heads-up display via a wireless link to her monitoring bracelet. She had already set this up to be transmitted in parallel to her primary care physician and dietician. For the rest of the drive, all four people interacted with their devices through voice, facial cues, and minimal finger inputs for another typical week in the Digital Swarm.

An Executive Day in the Life

Bob LeRoy had seen this before at Pharmaco. His youngest employees were finding ways to outmaneuver the old ways of doing things. But now they were armed with new technologies such as wireless networking that was making them even more agile and innovative compared to the rest of the company. They had already written several mash-ups using open-source code and their cognitive devices to sense the proximity of other salespeople, partners, existing and target physicians, and even competitor sales reps. Then they would optimize their routing in real time each day to maximize sales effectiveness. They were lapping the more experienced sales reps by selling as a self-organizing swarm versus more traditional serial sales call planning. In addition to more sales calls, they had a higher close rate due to their ability to connect with each target physician in a highly personalized way. For instance, one junior rep could determine if a given doctor was in surgery, relaxing in the lounge, seeing patients at his office, or out to lunch by tapping into the doctor's location-aware social networking profile. Armed with this information and being careful not to abuse it, this same rep could send the appropriate application, message, or survey to the doctor at the most appropriate time for him to consume it and potentially act on it.

As for Bob, his job as regional sales VP had been transformed dramatically through the latest wireless technology and applications. Instead of "riding shotgun" with sales reps to monitor progress, he could get almost real-time updates of their progress down to each call, including multimedia feeds of the actual sales discussion, assuming approval by the physician. This allowed Bob to concentrate on scanning the market for competitive products, new customer trends, and emerging market opportunities to focus his team's attention on. With access to his sales force, other employees, partners, and retailers as distributed sensors, Bob could receive a stream of market intelligence data. He could mine this data immediately using network-based computing resources, all accessible via his wireless device. In fact, Bob spends most of his time in his mobile home, moving from state to state, touring the country with his wife. Why not make the country your office if you can?

Scenario B: Killer Bees

"The future of mankind is a race between education and catastrophe."

—*H.G. Wells*

In this future, technology breakthroughs have a dark side. Mobile viruses spread through open wireless networks like a pandemic, infecting mobile devices throughout many parts of the developed world. User privacy is threatened constantly because mobile hijackers abound, taking advantage of the many network paths to access a user's device. This leads to "gated communities" in the wireless world to protect users as strong brands become the trusted brokers of transactions. Terrorists frequently use mobile devices to organize large-scale attacks. Biochips are even used to design pathogens such as a synthetic version of avian flu. Key wireless standards fracture along regional lines, and 4G wireless intellectual property becomes a veritable arms race among companies and countries. Wireless commerce struggles to meet the enormous market expectations once postulated by analysts. Secure broadband wireless is relegated to the rich as public WiFi projects become cesspools of illegal activities, leaving black eyes on cities and municipalities that once saw these projects as a path to economic growth. Artificial intelligence (AI) cannot deliver on the "device-centric" promise. Instead, the overwhelming technology numbs our ability to innovate.

The following sections describe the outcomes of each of the key variables in the Killer Bees scenario.

Network Trust

In the world of Killer Bees, technology, standards, and policy solutions have been unable to keep up with the increasing sophistication of wireless cyber-criminals and their tactics. The bad guys now see wireless networks, given their inherent connectedness, as the most effective medium for spreading malicious programs and gaining access to sensitive user information. This includes the biological spread of wireless worms, infecting and taking over devices to support large-scale attacks on protected networks (government, financial, healthcare, utilities). Governments and standards bodies are unable to align on common defense mechanisms, leaving organizations and network providers to invest in their own unique protection approach. This creates great disparities among secure and unsecure wireless networks, resulting in a "pay for protection" model for operators and their customers.

Technology Breakthroughs

While there have been pockets of progress in wireless technology and networking, there has been little progress in integrating these developments into real operational benefits for users and organizations. Improvements have been made in smart devices, wireless broadband speeds and coverage, and sensing networks. But interoperability has suffered from a lack of cooperation among standards groups, governments, and technology providers, keeping many breakthroughs from having a significant market impact. Many technology advancements that do happen are "off-the-market" inventions from subversive players seeking to undermine the establishment. This includes fourth-generation phreaking, in which existing smartphones are stripped and reprogrammed to increase performance, crack networks, and pirate wireless bandwidth and applications. Also, an array of custom gadgets are designed for clandestine and military applications where ad hoc wireless networks are used to support specific missions. For instance, low-cost dragonfly-size flying sensors are available to support everything from reconnaissance on drug smugglers to high-end personal security monitoring. The black market for wireless innovations is thriving. But in the consumer and business markets, wireless technology is not a bright spot, because true innovation fails to scale to the masses. Innovative apps and services stay confined to local markets and closed user communities.

Wireless Market Growth

The global wireless market is struggling to grow, falling far short of the lofty expectations set around 4G. A number of factors have been cited, including incompatible standards, battery-constrained device performance, and the lack of a killer app. Almost all of the developments at the handset, network, and application level have been incremental at best. Irrational exuberance caused several major carriers and new "big brand" entrants to overpay for the 4G spectrum. This forced them to write off significant losses, because most consumers are indifferent to the benefits of faster wireless networks without rich applications to run over them. Market growth has slowed to just a few percentage points per year and does not show any signs of picking up soon. Growth in developing markets has been a bit stronger, driven by the conversion of previously unserved consumers in the growing population.

Strength of Economy

The global economy has fallen into a malaise as terrorism, energy prices, and general economic and political conflict have created an enormous drag on progress. Even wireless, which was once ordained as a key catalyst for economic growth, has been unable to show real impact. It has become a communications medium plagued with reliability, security, and cost issues. Customers scrutinize their wireless spending and expect a lot for their dollar. As a result, wireless network operators, device vendors, and application developers must truly distinguish themselves to avoid being commoditized and thrown into a price war. There is also a clear distinction between the haves and the have-nots. Those who can afford the top-of-the-line smartphones and associated apps gain the benefits of 4G—at least locally. Many others remain at a basic 3G level of communications and networking.

Killer Applications

Applications for fourth-generation wireless networks generally have failed to really transform wireless usage. Service providers have had to clamp down on open development platforms due to the onslaught of network attacks resulting from vulnerabilities and malicious code introduced by some of these open-source apps. Maverick entrepreneurs and bold independent developers have been able to create applications for local communities and closed networks that have done well on a small scale. But very few applications have spread to a large segment of the wireless market base. Some local and community apps do find some success:

- **Mapping**—The ability to quickly plot the user's location onto a current, accurate map is now mainstream. New mapping includes larger databases of amenities, shopping, and group tracking.
- **Security/surveillance**—Municipal, community, company, and even individual security applications have sprouted up everywhere as the world has become one of both physical and virtual threats. With terrorism more prevalent than ever in developed regions of the world, those who can afford to purchase high-end sensor networks and personal "early warning" systems for their families and companies. These tools alert them to nearby threats such as biological agents and munitions.

- **Security/privacy management**—A range of software and service options on the market offer both proactive and defensive functions in protecting wireless users from malicious attacks or unwanted access to their personal information. The dramatic improvement in device intelligence and processing power is applied to detecting potentially threatening patterns. This can thwart possible attacks and also launch smart agents to test the integrity and security of wireless networks prior to their use. Security and privacy are a high-risk, high-stakes game. Again, the haves and have-nots are separated by significant capabilities to defend against threats.

- **People tracking**—The general state of paranoia in the Killer Bees future makes companies and individuals want to know the whereabouts and activities of key people. Mobile devices still have advanced location awareness capabilities, but they are used on an opt-in basis due to the privacy concerns mentioned earlier. "Big Brother" applications allow quick tracking of targeted people down to the submeter level. When device tracking is turned off, the service sends out alerts. The benefit is safety and productivity, as in the case of a sales force optimizing its coverage on sales calls for a local market. The downside is limited freedom to find personal time and space without being "watched" through the network.

Standards Alignment

Underhanded tactics and scandal have led to mistrust in many of the formal standards bodies governing the introduction of 4G wireless. What was once a strong GSM and CDMA standards foundation to build on has disintegrated into a faction of individual companies and their IP portfolios "buying" their way into specific standards. The United States and Europe move further apart as the mega wireless players on both sides of the Atlantic fail to reach agreement on sharing IP and promoting common standards. Meanwhile, specific markets like India, China, and Brazil are creating their own standards. This forces operators and vendors to buy in early at significant risk of having to develop and build nonstandard products for each specific market. Software-based devices have not kept pace with the large number of diverse wireless standards. Communication authorities like the FCC and ITU have trouble staying ahead of standards on allocating the wireless spectrum. Without significant progress on dynamic spectrum allocation, the number of interference complaints and spectrum lawsuits increases due to poor coordination. The lack of unity on standards results in higher-priced devices and base stations, enormous roaming fees, and a flattening of global wireless usage on the high end of the market.

Low-End Disruption

Growth at the high end of the market is suffering from broken standards and security threats. However, the low end continues to gain subscribers through basic services where simple voice and text can meet the communication needs of communities and regions. In this segment of the market, interoperability, high-end device features, and even security are not the key decision drivers for subscribers given their economic strata and basic application set. In particular, growth in the BRIC (Brazil, Russia, India, and China) countries and Africa is strongest where both direct and shared-use phones (multiple users per phone) penetrate more than 30% of the population.

Wireless Social Networks

In this future, wireless social networks go through a major trans-formation. The growth of mainstream social networks like MySpace and Facebook suffers as basic rules of interaction and etiquette are regularly violated. This creates mistrust across these networks and a "tragedy of the commons" effect. Irresponsible behaviors "poison the well" for the masses, causing an exodus from large national and global brands. Instead, people gravitate to smaller, more personalized local networks with strong privacy guarantees and clear rules of engage-ment. Some of these networks start to charge a fee to provide the active management and protection that users seek. Much like private country clubs, these networks have a lot of say in who joins, weeding out those who may not offer value to other members or who present a potential threat.

Seamless Mobility

Seamless mobility is still just an aspiration. Very little progress has been made toward filling in coverage gaps, supporting roaming between all levels of hot spots and the regional and national wireless networks of different providers. The financial incentives are not there to support these investments, and a weak global economy has hamstrung governments in footing the bill. Municipal wireless networks, once heralded as the pathway to universal wireless coverage and economic expansion, are routinely being dismantled and shut down due to poor economics, security holes, and lack of integration with more popular wireless networks.

Embedded Sensors

In the Killer Bees future, sensors continue to proliferate as Moore's Law remains intact and grain-sized microprocessors find their way into almost everything. The dilemma is that most of these remain unconnected or attached to local proprietary networks. The visions for smart homes, intelligent highways, and agile supply chains remain unfulfilled as piecemeal, vendor-centric wireless solutions compete and leave the hard integration tasks to the customer. Pockets of success exist in "closed-loop" sensor applications like package and baggage tracking, personal health monitoring, and the security/threat warning systems mentioned earlier.

Gen Z Dominance

Despite all the early hype, the Gen Z'ers have had little impact on the mainstream use of wireless and the emergence of new applications and devices. Their enthusiasm for actively networking with new users and promoting transparency in their personal activities wanes as they mature and face the realities of a more hostile wireless Internet and perverse, selfish behaviors that trump social responsibility. They become conformists as decision-makers and leaders in the workforce as opposed to the mavericks and pioneers they were once thought to be.

Distributed Authority

Employees still cling to organizations for a sense of belonging and the assurance of resources (including communication networks) to get things done. Small businesses and individuals don't always have this luxury in the Killer Bees world. However, strong trends around telecommuting and virtual offices still stretch the current organizational structure. CIOs are in a better position to control these extended resources through central policies and procedures given the high-risk environment for companies. While some organizations flatten, others move toward a strong oversight model with employee tracking, virtual private networks, and approved application sets and networks. All changes to general policies are piloted and thoroughly fleshed out before being launched across a given organization.

Cognitive Devices

Handsets and other wireless devices have progressed to the point of being "micro-supercomputers" with processing power easily exceeding that of the human brain. The "power in your palm" is incredible. You can make scheduling decisions in the background; check the security/privacy status of different networks; track the proximity of groups, individuals, traffic, and locations of interest; and make real-time routing decisions. All this helps you lead a more productive and safe life. The software updating of new wireless standards and interoperability features has been very limited due to the battle among standards groups, including the technology vendors (who develop the devices and associated software). While radios are certainly "cognitive," they are far from fully dynamic, with interoperation limited to only a few standards. Some frustrated researchers write their own patch code to have phones and devices work with different networks, sometimes called phreaking. But this is a high-risk solution for those looking to gain security/privacy protection from the same networks they are trying to circumvent.

Privacy/Security Concerns

Security and privacy are at the center of major political and commercial debates. Privacy advocates are waging war on the large wireless network carriers and Internet portals, claiming that they are not doing enough on their own dime to fix what has become an epidemic of security and privacy breaches. Some very visible mishaps have raised the bar even higher, including the loss of 50 million health records via a wireless network security hole. Denial-of-service attacks have taken on a new form. Thousands to millions of wireless devices are affected by the fast spread of software agents using the intelligence of new devices for malicious purposes by taking over their decision-making logic. These attacks can now disrupt everything from port security to supply chains due to their critical dependency on wireless networks.

Health and Environmental Concerns

Several high-profile deaths and illnesses linked to cell phone and wireless networks have put the industry under a watchful eye. A class-action lawsuit is initiated by plaintiffs led by two high-profile celebrities. Their 12-year-old daughter has been diagnosed with brain cancer, and scientists have drawn a compelling link between wireless devices, cell phone tower radiation, and cancer. This has created a tenuous situation for operators and device manufacturers, who are already bleeding from 4G investment write-downs and weak subscriber revenue growth. Ironically, the cost of their defense has been passed back to users in the form of increased monthly charges and lower subsidies on devices. The disposal of billions of cell phone batteries has also become a toxic cleanup issue, with reports of groundwater contamination and children's health disorders. Although cell

phones do provide health monitoring as a benefit to those who can
afford it, they are known equally as chief polluters and threats to the
environment. The emergence of new "eco-friendly" wireless services
and brands (some backed by existing carriers) shakes up the marketplace by taking advantage of the built-up frustration and perception
of irresponsibility among the traditional wireless players.

A Consumer Day in the Life

Margaret Shuster walked into the Kingston Mall with her 14-year-
old daughter, Natalie. She reminded Natalie to check the network
access and security settings on her smartphone, because their
neighbor's identity recently was hijacked via a mobile worm attack
on an unregistered network. Margaret took a quick look at the
retail routing map based on her shopping preferences maintained
in a secure profile by her wireless carrier, Vizcom, for a premium
fee. She asked the mobile concierge to also include Natalie's shopping preferences in the retail navigation service. After Natalie gave
permission to access her profile, a primary and alternative route
came up for navigating the mall, considering both time constraints
(based on typical store wait times) and mall traffic. Before she
selected the course she and Natalie would take through the mall,
Margaret quickly jumped onto her "Home-eyes" surveillance service to check on their pets and also make sure the air-conditioning
was turned down. Natalie was busy punching away on her private
messaging service. She dropped her Facebook and IM services
almost two years ago due to several threatening attacks to corrupt
her profile. She now uses the closed network messaging service
offered by their wireless carrier. Even though it does not work with
all her friends' mobile devices, it beats e-mail.

Margaret and Natalie set off on a brisk walk through the mall. Both
had their ear inserts and hidden mics in place in case a new call
came in or they needed to use voice response to a text message.
Fears of brain cancer still linger, because several recent cases have
been written up in the *New England Journal of Medicine*. Life is
interesting, to say the least. Wireless is very much a part of their
lives. But the risk of communicating seems to be going up each day.

An Executive Day in the Life

Fred Lundy had been on sales calls all day. He was incredulous that he was still experiencing dropped calls in this day and age. Twice he got cut off on critical sales calls that may have cost him his quarterly bonus. He thought about switching carriers, but he probably did not have enough pull, because his CIO had just switched the company wireless plan to Onetouch for cost and security reasons. Fred's company recently was attacked by a vicious wireless virus that spread from an external partner network into the company's most secure data networks. It compromised key customer and financial information, costing the company tens of millions of dollars. As a result, the newly appointed CIO was not about to take any chances. He moved forward on a new carrier agreement and a draconian wireless policy for employees. Despite all the capability available through the latest mobile devices and applications, they could use only the bare minimum set of applications beyond voice. Even the use of corporate WiFi networks was limited to secure voice and data connections. Home wireless networks required special corporate approval and typically also required special encryption keys for remote access to the company network.

What used to be a flexible workweek had become a fairly rigid routine of required office time to take care of secure activities that could no longer be done easily on the road. Fred's company recently discussed the idea of employee location tracking for the "benefit" of employees. Against significant opposition, the company now was piloting this application with several branch office sites. In addition, the company had reigned in many of its web service applications to just a few large vendors managing secure data centers. Even when employees had a better way to do something via wireless, it was tough to move the organization to experiment, given the low trust in most wireless networks and the broader Internet. Fred thought about the company's need to expand in emerging markets, because the U.S. and European markets had become saturated with their industrial controls products. He feared that if they didn't get there soon, the low-end innovation from these countries would eventually find its way back as an attractive solution for established markets. But how could he sell into BRIC countries without reliable wireless connectivity and access to key corporate product information? Fred scratched his head and started for home, hoping he would be able to chat with his branch in Singapore later that night on a personal VoIP connection.

Key Insight

The unwired future could present both significant opportunities and threats for organizations and individuals. Leadership foresight, adaptive planning, and organizational agility will be critical to thrive in the Digital Swarm.

These vastly different scenarios, Nature Aligns and Killer Bees, provide possibilities for how the 4G future could play out. However, they certainly are not exhaustive. The implications of these different worlds could be dramatic for both organizations and individuals.

4

The Swarm Effect: Implications for You and Your Company

"In the future, the learners will inherit the Earth, while the learned will find themselves beautifully equipped to live in a world that no longer exists."

—*Eric Hoffer, philosopher*

This chapter examines the implications of the alternative unwired futures discussed in Chapter 3 for both individuals and organizations. The implications are evaluated by geography, industry sector, and segment of the wireless value chain. Examples are given of companies that are at the leading edge. This chapter looks at where value is likely to be created and destroyed, and who would be the likely winners and losers in each scenario. The disruptive potential of different emerging technologies and business models is also assessed. This should provide important insights for leaders trying to figure out where to place their bets on potential wireless partners and wirelessly enabled products and services.

The future scenarios discussed in the preceding chapter represent a variety of outcomes that must be considered. Even though they share some similarities, the differences are stark, especially in the areas of privacy, trust, networks, services, and the behavior of key actors. Who will win in the delivery of wireless services and applications? Let's explore both future scenarios to see what happens to the playing field.

Figure 4.1 shows the relative increase and decrease in market power of key players in the wireless ecosystem in a Nature Aligns future.

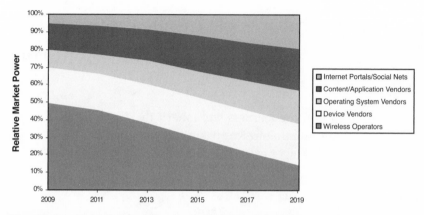

Figure 4.1   Relative market power in the Nature Aligns scenario

Network operators lose power as it shifts to owners of popular applications and content as well as end users. Due to the emergence of intelligent devices and "user-centric" networks, traditional operators have lots of competition and can no longer extract a high premium for their wireless "pipes." Mobile virtual network operators (MVNOs) that are not burdened by owning infrastructure make significant progress, backed by Internet portals and social networking platforms.

Figure 4.2 shows the relative increase and decrease in market power of key players in the wireless ecosystem for a Killer Bees future.

Network operators increase their power as wireless services move toward a "gated community" model. Applications, content, operating systems, portals, and device vendors all have to pay a toll to ride on the most secure, highest-performance highways. The breakdown in

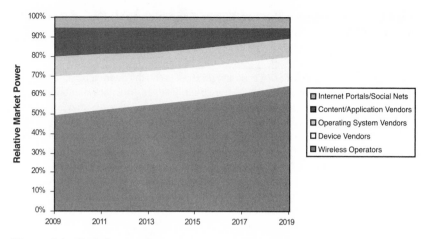

Figure 4.2   Relative market power in the Killer Bees scenario

> ## Key Insight
>
> Market power may shift significantly between wireless operators, device and operating system vendors, content providers, application developers, and Internet portals, depending on which future scenario emerges. Flexible partnerships will be critical for companies trying to drive a successful wireless strategy.

open standards and interoperability has forced these same dependent players to choose the networks they support and align with strategically, resulting in fewer options for end users. So depending on which scenario emerges, the players driving the market and gaining the greatest share of profits will differ greatly.

How do these future scenarios project to different geographies? How do the scenarios play out in different industry sectors beyond the communications sector? Table 4.1 compares the implications of each future scenario for different geographies and industry sectors.

TABLE 4.1   Comparing the Two Future Scenarios for Different Regions and Industries

Region	Nature Aligns	Killer Bees
North America	North America is no longer the most attractive wireless market in terms of total revenue, but it is still very profitable and has become the most dynamic in terms of new entrants. American consumer products and retailers have become some of the most innovative and progressive users of wireless in their business models.	North America benefits from its historic lack of integration among wireless standards as proprietary networks and gated communities become the norm to protect against persistent threats. U.S. companies are also leaders in wireless security hardware and software, although much of this does not get exported due to decreased trade and cooperation around the globe.
Latin America	The level of healthcare improves dramatically in places like Brazil, Venezuela, and Peru. The spread of diseases is tracked, people are quarantined much faster, and patients in remote villages can be diagnosed via a mobile device.	Drug rings and other subversive groups exert control over governments and markets by leveraging advanced reconnaissance and wireless cyber attacks and by maintaining private, protected networks for their own communications. Dictatorships become strengthened as people turn to the government for protection and opposition groups are less able to organize. Corruption reigns supreme as the elite look to preserve and widen the wealth gap.

TABLE 4.1   Comparing the Two Future Scenarios for Different Regions and Industries

Region	Nature Aligns	Killer Bees
Europe/Middle East	There is complete convergence of communications and media accessible via mobile devices across all of Europe. The Scandinavian countries continue to be trailblazers in the development of open platforms and devices and a live lab for mobile social applications. Budding economic zones like Dubai have embedded wireless into everything, enabling a true context-aware, interactive experience everywhere you go.	The rapid proliferation of viruses and worms across European wireless networks has caused a rethink of common standards such as Bluetooth that magnified the threat. Traditional operators offer multi-level security for a price in order to maintain their best customers. The teen and lower-income segments are relegated to communication "back alleys." Terrorist groups gain strength in the Middle East and elsewhere through wirelessly enabled communities of extremists. Very few watchdogs can track and monitor them across disparate networks.
Asia	Asia leads the way on the most advanced gadgets, applications, and services due to an insatiable appetite for cool products and virtual entertainment. However, much of the intelligence in the phones and applications comes from Western R&D, with favorable licensing agreements with Asian suppliers to access the world's largest markets. Almost all activities are performed via wireless devices and peripherals. In Japan, wallets have all but disappeared with the complete penetration of secure mobile e-wallets.	Asia's progressive stance on wireless applications has begun to backfire as users opt for trust and safety over cool and adventurous games and devices. Major manufacturers learn to adapt to service these new market needs while upstart providers struggle for credibility. Countries like China commonly have "lockdowns" on specific networks, limiting the flow of external traffic on national networks.

TABLE 4.1   Comparing the Two Future Scenarios for Different Regions and Industries

Region	Nature Aligns	Killer Bees
Africa	Africa has been the beneficiary of enormous technology and infrastructure investments as stability has made the region a viable and cheaper alternative to Chinese outsourcing. Almost all communications infrastructure is wireless since very few wires existed before. Africa has become a poster child for community-based innovation using wireless services and devices in everything from distributed financial services and retail to supply chain and energy management.	Africa has become a cesspool of "infected" networks. Much of the great progress in microfinance, virtual markets, and remote healthcare has been undone by subversive activities such as the theft and misuse of financial and personal information. Although the market is still growing, Africa has regressed, with only the elite having access to advanced wireless capabilities.

Industry	Nature Aligns	Killer Bees
Manufacturing	Factory floors and distribution centers have become completely automated and flexible "shells" as wireless allows for rapid reconfiguration of intelligent equipment. Wireless sensors allow products to be tracked, shipped, and stocked at an individual item level versus a SKU or pallet level, allowing for real-time, dynamic supply chains.	Factory floors and warehouses have evolved little in the last decade, because wireless standards have not converged, and automated equipment tends to be linked to a specific proprietary standard. Due to high rates of theft and piracy, products are tracked using wireless networks, but at a high cost, because proprietary device/tag prices are still relatively high as a percentage of product cost.

TABLE 4.1   Comparing the Two Future Scenarios for Different Regions and Industries

Industry	Nature Aligns	Killer Bees
Energy	Proactive energy monitoring and management have become the norm, with cell phones at the core. Consumers and businesses can actively trade kilowatt-hours of local generation or shift their energy load to more cost-effective times with simple commands from their mobile device.	Some progress has been made on wireless meter reading as a cost savings for utilities. But little integration of energy management and information with communications has occurred, other than a few niche applications. People can check surveillance cameras and the status of lights and appliances through a private Web site, but not their meters. The energy companies have not made this information available on the Internet due to security concerns.
Healthcare	Patients have universal and portable access to healthcare information anytime they need it, enabling specialized medicine and more effective disease prevention and management. Wireless is leveraged extensively in connecting devices and monitoring nodes within and across patients to medical providers.	Significant backlash has occurred against healthcare information and device companies. Biochips and implants have become targets for theft of patient information and even financial information, because these devices connect to other private wireless networks. The lack of universal wireless standards has limited the ability of full-scale remote healthcare solutions.

TABLE 4.1   Comparing the Two Future Scenarios for Different Regions and Industries

Industry	Nature Aligns	Killer Bees
Financial services	Secure and open access to financial records across institutions allows customers to optimize their financial services and allows non-traditional players to compete with new, innovative wireless services. Legacy exchanges like the NYSE and LSE continue to lose power as once closely held institutional information is available to the general investor. Individual and community-based hedge funds spring up and thrive on the back of transparent fund structures and published track records.	Wireless banking and e-wallet have had only modest penetration, with private solutions offered by the major carriers. Customers still prefer dealing with tellers. Lots of investment and effort are put into tracking "bad guys" and abnormal flows of money. Several major markets (NYSE, CME) had to shut down when wide-scale denial-of-service attacks (both wireless and wireline) hit their systems. Proprietary software vendors sell surveillance platforms.
Retail	Due to effective privacy protection standards, retailers can offer ultimate personalization using location-aware advertising and shopping advisors with everything from dietary advice to product comparisons based on proximity. Two-way, low-cost wireless sensors allow for dynamic tagging/pricing of every product in a retail store or outlet based on demand versus inventory. Brick-and-mortar stores become "demo centers" as most people make their final purchase virtually from their device after scanning for the best deal.	Wireless tagging of products and in-store product advice via mobile phones has been effective, but wide-scale location-aware shopping and advice have been shelved due to customers' privacy concerns. The hostile security environment has limited the deployment of wireless enablement in retail. Even some automated checkout machines have been foiled by wireless attackers. The cashless society is still not a reality.

TABLE 4.1   Comparing the Two Future Scenarios for Different Regions and Industries

Industry	Nature Aligns	Killer Bees
Media/ publishing	Mobile virtual reality capability has broken through into mass-market products, enabling a new wave of entertainment and games like virtual casinos and amusement parks. Authors and artists can openly create and publish under both public and private labels without fearing that their content will be pirated broadly. Record and publishing companies have either faded away or transformed themselves into community-based markets for new content where listeners decide whether an artist should be played or shelved.	Video and music piracy are common. Artists have started to publish work on specific private carrier networks, where the use of their content can be tracked so that they can earn some royalties. Nontraditional advertising, including mobile, makes modest headway. TV still dominates viewing habits. E-readers have penetrated the market, but the download speeds are slow enough to be a nuisance for users. Carriers and large brands still dominate the landscape as they provide basic and premium user protection on their network for an additional fee.
Professional services	Highly effective mobile knowledge management and telepresence applications have transformed professional services into a virtual delivery model. Due to the impact of immersive online education and anywhere access to expert systems, young consultants, lawyers, and accountants reach a partner level of proficiency within five years. This creates extremely flat, competitive organizations.	Professional services firms stick to fairly traditional deployment models as most of the highly virtual work gets scaled back. Clients do not want their networks accessed outside of their company borders, and they limit wireless deployments to very specific groups (such as sales and IT). Some more progressive firms get accused of tracking their employees via wireless location.

TABLE 4.1   Comparing the Two Future Scenarios for Different Regions
and Industries

Industry	Nature Aligns	Killer Bees
Aerospace/ defense	Terrorism has been marginalized by vigilant communities of global citizens pushing a peaceful and socially responsible agenda. Anomalous behavior is flagged and reported from the many "eyes" wandering the unwired world. Traditional defense contractors have repurposed much of their sensing and simulation technology to business and consumer applications requiring surveillance and protection.	The military use of wireless far outpaces anything in the commercial world, because leading-edge applications such as insect-sized sensors and secure mobile ad hoc networking are still cost-prohibitive for typical consumer markets. So although the battlefield is completely unwired, the home and office are still trying to cutting the cord.
Government	Governments regularly tap into wireless social networks or "smart mobs" to gather public opinion on pending legislation, mock voting, and even campaign activities. Emergency response and disaster relief have become highly coordinated across participating entities through standardized wireless and location-tracking solutions. Intelligent highways, traffic management, and transportation systems have emerged, with low-cost, distributed wireless sensors everywhere. There is not much the government doesn't know, but people know just as much about the government, maintaining an information power balance.	Governments get out of the wireless business after the massive failure of municipal WiFi projects. Despite widespread privacy and security issues, the government pushes the problem back on industry to solve, resulting in a gap between those who can afford protection and those who cannot. Most government activities are still done through live contact because the promise of virtual, extended government has waned due to lack of trust. Surveillance and monitoring activities continue to be a top priority as both foreign and domestic threats continue to pop up. Many schools ban wireless devices from classrooms to avoid compromising internal networks.

Even though it may appear that Killer Bees is a more constrained environment for growth, both scenarios create winners who can anticipate unique profit opportunities and exploit them with the appropriate business models.

Key Insight

Opportunities can be exploited in both future scenarios. Organizations must decide where to commit and where to stay flexible in order to maximize their overall Digital Swarm opportunity while minimizing their exposure.

These opportunities may vary by industry and geography across both scenarios, presenting a range of options for organizations to pursue, depending on which future emerges. In addition to scenarios and industry-specific strategies, common future success strategies will likely define winners in all industries across the globe. These options and success strategies are discussed in the next chapter.

5

Organizing for Success: Strategies and Options

"When it comes to the future, there are three kinds of people: those who let it happen, those who make it happen, and those who wonder what happened."

—*John M. Richardson, Jr.*

Just when we think we have the future figured out, it changes on us. This chapter describes success strategies that companies must follow to thrive in the new unwired environment. Because we don't know what that environment may look like, we can use future scenarios as a way to "bound" the range of future environments we could face. The goal in using scenarios is to be "roughly right" versus "precisely wrong." This chapter explores the use of future scenarios to challenge and develop business strategies to harness the Digital Swarm and drive a competitive advantage in your future markets.

Core and Contingent Strategies

To position your organization for success no matter what future emerges, you need to identify core strategies, which may pay off across many futures, and contingent strategies, which may pay off in only a specific future. Figure 5.1 illustrates this concept.

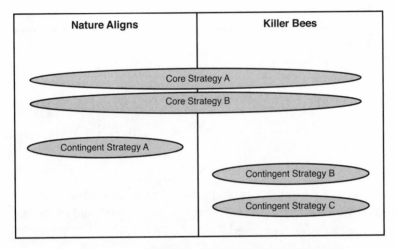

Figure 5.1   Core and contingent strategies across scenarios

Key Insight

Your wireless strategy should be a mix of core strategies that pay off no matter what future emerges and contingent strategies that pay off big in a specific future scenario.

Core strategies should have high investment priority, because they should benefit you in all scenarios. Contingent strategies dictate a staged investment approach, where commitment is increased as a specific future emerges.

Online Retailer Strategy Example

You are an online retailer with a global footprint. You're facing an uncertain future around wireless and the impact on your business. What different wireless strategies should you consider to win in the different markets you compete in?

For mature markets like North America, Europe, and Asia, in Nature Aligns you could take advantage of wide-scale acceptance of e-commerce, e-wallet, and mobile advertising as ways to stretch the shopping experience across the full work-life continuum. With dramatic improvements in context-aware mobile devices with immersive virtual reality (VR) user interfaces, the live experience of brick-and-mortar stores is not as unique and appealing as it once was. So ensuring that all products are accessible in VR form for demos will be a key to increasing sales. Also, "reality mining" will be critical to breaking through the massive amount of noise and personal decision filters in getting the right message to key customers. Reality mining means being able to access and mine customer behavior across many domains, including those connected through wireless networks. Owning the network is not nearly as critical as owning the most comprehensive profile of each customer.

For emerging markets like Asia, Latin America, and Africa, in Nature Aligns, having shopping apps that work on both basic (voice/text) and advanced cognitive handsets, as well as village/community-based shopping models, would provide a competitive edge. On the back end of the business, having an in-region manufacturing and distribution capability to take advantage of Africa and Latin America as the new low-cost producers in the world would provide significant economic leverage. Distributed healthcare, financial services, and retail applications such as microloans, virtual marketplace/auctions, and telehealth will also command a premium in these markets, because local merchants and buyers may still be in remote, hard-to-get-to locations.

In the Killer Bees future for mature markets, your market and operational strategies need to be prepared for the many threats to free commerce and must focus on building trust with customers. You may need to offer financial guarantees and insurance concerning the loss of customer data to show you are committed to protecting their information. Given the volatility in this future, consumers will seek safe havens in both the cyber and physical worlds. In the cyber world, they will look for trusted brands and private networks where they know their personal data is safe. If you cannot provide and manage this type of wireless and web infrastructure, you will need to partner with recognized brands that can. This may cost you, but you need your e-commerce site to be viewed as protected, or you may end up out of business.

People will also seek out comfortable retail outlets as a "cheap escape" from the threats around them, especially since they are not likely to travel as far for entertainment. This means that having a brick-and-mortar presence, either directly or through partnerships, will be critical to access this window where people are willing to spend on themselves. Because technology has continued to advance, especially smart mobile devices, there will be great opportunities to provide secure concierge-type services. With these services, customers get real-time shopping advice (price and performance comparisons, dietary info, inventory info) based on their exact location in the store. Your mobile concierge could also tell them if an online purchase would be more economical and time-efficient for a given item, factoring in the prices and waiting time in the store.

In emerging markets, online retail will morph rapidly in a Killer Bees future as transaction volumes grow but values remain relatively small, with a virtually nonexistent luxury segment due to economic pressures. High-end customers shop exclusively on private networks where security is guaranteed by large providers. At the low and middle ends of the market, people frequently switch wireless accounts and use prepaid services out of fear that their personal data will get stolen. This means that your traditional customer segmentation and targeting methods will need to be much more dynamic. Customers who can afford it will opt to carry secure ID cards that authenticate them for accessing private networks. Even if they switch mobile phones, these cards can be used to identify them. But this will require you to cut agreements with the large network operators that have significant leverage as a sole gateway to the customer. Low-end customers will be forced to live with a crapshoot approach to buying things securely. As a consequence, new models will emerge where purchases can still be made online via mobile devices. However, payment will be made at the local or village level and reconciled via a secure micropayments network run by one of the large carriers. Products are still shipped after payment is verified. Once again, the regional wireless carriers can demand a significant transaction fee due to the value of the secure private network they operate.

The strategies recommended for your online retail business so far have been more future scenario- or segment-specific. Here are some core strategies that would help you across all future scenarios and segments:

- **An intelligent, agile supply chain with wireless devices** embedded in all products to optimize inventory down to the item level. This will also require access to private networks and secure data management.

- **Location-aware advertising and product offerings** will need to be tailored to the store level, with additional privacy/security measures for the Killer Bees scenario.

- **Dynamic pricing based on local demand** and environmental factors. Low-cost two-way tagging will enable much more efficient inventory management in physical stores. Local demand information can be aggregated and applied to offers via online stores as well, whether connected to brick-and-mortar stores.

- **Technology co-development and risk sharing** with both device vendors and network operators to prepare for frequent disruptive changes in technology platforms.

- **User-centric online store development.** Having an online test lab where users can interact, check compatibility with new devices and browsers, download new viewing/virtual reality applications, test shopping and security features, and provide feedback on potential improvements.

Chemical Company Strategy Example

You are a multinational chemical company that is facing an uncertain future around wireless. You may need to consider a number of different strategies to win in the different markets you compete in.

In a Nature Aligns scenario, for mature markets like North America and Europe, you will need to find ways to differentiate yourself by leveraging wireless because many of the other best practices in your industry have been commoditized. One opportunity is transforming your sales force into an interconnected, adaptive organization. Key priorities and targets are continually assessed against knowledge and expertise to deploy resources and respond to customer needs in the most optimal way possible. This includes sales routing and product and pricing decisions. It also includes messaging and timing based on the location of individual sales reps and customers, what their own mobile devices are sensing in their activities that day, and matching solutions to needs. While much of the network service is available to support this, the central data warehouse and analytics for real-time decisioning would be specific to your company and customers. Your customers can be provided with tools accessible via mobile devices that allow them to quickly understand the pros and cons of using various chemicals in their finished products with virtual reality product configurators. For both security and efficiency reasons, intelligent tagging of both ingredients and products has become almost mandatory for players in developed markets. But also for supply chain monitoring, the interaction with these tags can be used to drive enormous gains in operational efficiency if mined for insights around the actual path an ingredient or product takes through the production and distribution stages, all the way through shipping, storage, and local distribution. To take advantage of this new level of supply chain intelligence, you can build manufacturing and distribution centers as flexible shells instead of rigid configurations. This allows for adaptation to improvements and changes in your process from factory to market. As open R&D (sourcing ideas from outside the company) becomes a necessary part of the corporate R&D portfolio, wireless can be used as a turbocharger to boost interactions among scientists, engineers, and product developers across different locations and domains. For instance, process engineers can brainstorm and exchange 3D sketches as they traverse a manufacturing facility and communicate with a venture-backed factory automation start-up on the other side of the world about possible solutions.

For emerging markets in a Nature Aligns future, it will be critical that you can quickly collect information on the key players and monitor their activities. These key players include regulators, suppliers, customers, competitors, and new entrants who can impact the market. Leveraging ubiquitous wireless networks, you could use your partners and suppliers as sensors to pick up new signals faster, especially in regions where public data is hard to get or not very accurate. This will be key, because the emerging markets have the fastest-growing economies, and new applications will spring up for chemically based products almost daily. But just as frequently, regulations and rules will change, such as environmental requirements, which could cause you to rethink certain product approaches. Africa, in particular, has risen to become a significant outsourced manufacturer for the chemical industry, but challenges remain to integrate across various business rules and policies in different African nations. Again, market agility is the key, and wireless can be a key enabler for creating a competitive advantage in this area.

In a Killer Bees future, you will need to be keenly aware of security risks in the markets you operate in. You also will need strong on-the-ground intelligence to drive decisions at local and regional levels as markets become more specialized. The challenge is that networks are not seamlessly connected, so much of your intelligence network will need to have access to secure private networks to relay information. This may require special investments in dedicated network access and encryption. In addition, physical security is a major concern at both manufacturing and distribution facilities in emerging markets. Low-cost surveillance solutions will be in demand. Wireless and IP video will provide distributed "eyes" around each facility, with the capability to mine video files for anomalies and send alerts to the mobile devices of key personnel. In case of chemical or biological emergencies or attacks, the surveillance network and employee devices could be equipped with biochemical threat sensors to detect and report potentially dangerous levels. Product counterfeiting has also become a major threat and liability for your company. Wireless tags will be needed to validate ingredient and product integrity at various checkpoints, with wireless sensors allowing for flexibility in where the checkpoints can be. Last, because emerging markets are still stuck in 2G and 3G wireless technology in many cases, your communication approaches will need to be adjusted to the market. You will need the capacity to develop wireless customer and market innovations that may need only basic text and voice versus more elaborate multimedia or VR functions.

Besides these strategies, which are geared at specific future market conditions and regions, your chemical company could pursue strategies that should pay off in all future scenarios and segments:

- **Intelligence gathering using wireless-enabled networks** including employees, partners, customers, suppliers, and third-party information sources to quickly sense changes in market conditions.

- **An empowered sales force** with full wireless access to market intelligence, updates from other sales reps, and real-time pricing/product decisioning.

- **Wireless-enabled flexible factory and distribution center configurations,** where product manufacturing and distribution processes can be easily redesigned for efficiency gains and also to adapt to new market requirements and regulations.

- **Wireless productivity tools for employees,** allowing them to easily pull down rich media training and instruction materials, standard forms, customer profiles, and technical support info via their mobile devices. These can be remotely updated at any time.

Common Wireless Success Factors

Every organization, like the online retailer and chemical company examples you just read about, will have a unique set of core and contingent strategies. These will be based on the organization's industry dynamics and wireless intensity, geographic footprint, and operating model. However, common capabilities exist that would pay off for any organization trying to compete in the range of unwired futures and in response to emerging 4G trends. Based on looking at early innovators and assessing winning attributes across future scenarios, industries, and geographies, ten common success factors have been identified that can help you adapt and win:

- **Wireless savvy/literacy**—The percentage of employees who own latest-generation wireless devices and subscribe to latest-generation wireless services
- **Wireless broadband access**—The penetration of wireless broadband among employees for accessing work applications
- **Wireless innovation**—The percentage of new products and services that leverage wireless as an enabler or delivery medium
- **Organizational authority**—The extent to which decision-making authority in the organization is distributed (peer-to-peer) versus centralized (hierarchical)
- **Wireless ecosystem**—The overall percentage of employees, customers, partners, and vendors who actively connect, communicate, and transact with each other through a wireless network
- **Wireless technology**—The rate at which wireless technology and applications are updated/refreshed with the latest versions
- **Wireless content**—The percentage of your organization's content that is geared toward an immersive wireless experience
- **Wireless interconnectedness**—The level of seamless interconnectivity between your wireless users and your organization's other networks
- **Wireless mass collaboration**—The extent to which the organization uses text messaging, IM, blogs, and wikis accessed via wireless handhelds to communicate and organize initiatives
- **Wireless social networking**—The extent to which your employees use wireless for social networking to accomplish higher-level goals beyond just work (relationship building, charity, entertainment)

Each of these success factors is discussed in more detail, along with a world-class organization example, in the following sections.

Wireless Savvy/Literacy

An organization with high wireless savvy and literacy is one in which most employees not only use the latest generation of wireless devices and services, but also use advanced wireless to improve their personal effectiveness. These organizations ensure that their employees are fully equipped to use wireless as a competitive differentiator in how they do business. Today, this includes networks, smart devices, and peripherals, with 3G, WiFi, and Bluetooth moving toward 4G wireless technology in the future. An organization that embodies wireless savvy is the U.S. Military Special Forces. Every activity is directed via wireless connectivity, and each soldier can use a variety of radios and even commercial technologies (such as BlackBerries) to accomplish his mission.

Wireless Broadband Access

Wireless broadband access with speeds approaching residential broadband (over 1Mbps) enables a whole new set of applications for the unwired enterprise. These may include mobile videoconferencing, access to critical multimedia content, product demos, decision-support applications, productivity and creativity tools, and enterprise platform access. An example of an organization that provides this level of wireless support is the Florida Public School System, the seventh largest public school system in the United States. Recently it rolled out broadband wireless on 234 campuses, with 5,500 access points connecting over 40,0000 wireless-enabled laptops and devices.[1] This will drive more efficient and economic operation of the schools and a superior, innovative learning experience for both students and teachers.

Wireless Innovation

There is tremendous opportunity when using wireless as an innovation platform, yet very few companies have moved in this direction to date. Great opportunities will exist to drive more innovation with emerging 4G wireless technologies. These might include scouting for new product and service opportunities via wireless-enabled networks; using wireless to pilot and get feedback on new products; and supporting the rollout, targeted marketing, and sales support effort for a new product or service. Ember has built power-ful wireless sensor network solutions for energy management and building automation based on standards such as Zigbee. It is addressing an enormous demand in the market for energy efficiency by using wireless to interconnect previously disparate elements in buildings (appliances, metering, HVAC, controls). This has resulted in greater intelligence and decision-making.

Organizational Authority

The more distributed the organization and its decision-making capability, the greater the impact of wireless networks on driving real business benefit. Flat organizations allow individuals to easily connect to many networks (enterprise, supplier, customer, professional, per-sonal). People can harness the intelligence and knowledge in those net-works along with situational information to drive context-relevant, real-time decisions. With rigid hierarchies, these networks will be much less fluid and more difficult to connect to achieve rich context and optimal decisions. A great example of an organization that operates in a flat hierarchy is Google. Its employees may select what projects they choose to work on for a significant portion of their workweek. This includes wireless innovations such as Google's wireless phone concept (GPhone) and its open wireless operating system (Android). These self-forming teams are very much interconnected across Google's cam-pus wireless network to collaborate and push new ideas forward.

Wireless Ecosystem

Wireless ecosystems are formed when multiple organizations interconnect their activities via wireless to achieve mutually beneficial objectives. This interconnection can be through a variety of wireless networks and devices or a single standard. The impor-tant measurement of the value in an ecosystem is the balanced exchange of information and business value among players in the ecosystem. The University of Washington has been a pioneer in experimenting with wireless ecosystems. It created them by attaching wireless RFID tags to everything from equipment to people and their personal items. This made it possible to mine for patterns of interaction and behaviors useful to improving the use of wireless in social settings.[2] Major retailers like Wal-Mart and organizations like the Department of Defense have driven mandates on the use of wireless tags by their partners and vendors to improve supply chain agility and intelligence.

Wireless Technology

Changing technology platforms usually is a huge risk for most enterprises, especially given the typical switching costs for large enterprise solutions. To protect against this risk, enterprises have invested $5,000 to $7,500 per access point (footnote) in custom wireless solutions that are tailored to their business. The challenge is that for an emerging technology area like next-generation wireless, they will be stuck using an uncompetitive platform, because new players can start with cheaper, next-generation solutions. With the standardization of wireless technologies, there may be less risk in using commercially available solutions versus proprietary ones. This is especially true when the technology can be configured remotely or can be easily refreshed, as with smart, software-based devices. FedEx is a great example of a company that is constantly leveraging the latest wireless platforms to drive new applications for its business, both customer-facing and operational applications. It has migrated from proprietary platforms to more commercially available wireless solutions to focus more on business applications and less on the network/infrastructure development.

Wireless Content

Making the company's content available in rich, immersive formats via wireless devices has been a challenge for many companies, especially traditional content providers. Whether it's the feeling of watching a big screen, reading a book, or talking to other people, doing these through a wireless device has never felt authentic. Yet some leading-edge examples have taken the wireless multimedia experience to a new level. The Kindle e-book reader from Amazon is a great example of replicating the traditional experience of reading via a wireless device. Kindle uses E-Ink technology to achieve the feel of real pages (texture, ink quality, page rendering) so that users get the sense that they are reading a book or newspaper. Attaching this to Amazon's book library via a broadband wireless network provides universal, on-demand reading. Apple is another company that has managed to take the experience of listening to music to an "anywhere experience," expanding this to video and allowing content updates via wireless networks.

Wireless Interconnectedness

To achieve true ubiquitous broadband communications and interactivity, wireless networks need to connect seamlessly with each other, making handoffs invisible to the user. This concept is built in to some of the 4G wireless solutions being considered. However, it is not a feature of all current wireless networking platforms, such as 2G and 3G cellular standards, WiFi variants, short-range wireless technologies like Bluetooth, and even cordless phones and fixed-line networks. As part of an effort called Fixed Mobile Convergence (FMC), a number of vendors are offering special devices. They can switch between several wireless and wireline networks, depending on which one may be best (from a cost and/or quality perspective) for the user at a given location. Ford Motor Company and MGM Mirage Hotels and Casinos are two companies that have increased interconnectivity among key employees by deploying some of these early FMC solutions.

Wireless Mass Collaboration

Unlocking the power of wireless to drive collaboration and action among large numbers of people could present a market changing opportunity for companies that can pull it off. We have already seen major social networking platforms like MySpace and Facebook transition to wireless as a primary form of interaction. Through these platforms, users can interact and self-organize around interests very easily. Chapter 1 mentioned how the Philippine government was overthrown by smart mobs equipped with basic cell phone texting. There are also the dark examples of drug dealers using disguised prepaid cell phones to manage their supply chains and al-Qaeda using encrypted wireless devices to coordinate terrorist activities. But probably the most popular example of using wireless to gather input from the masses is *American Idol*, which collects votes from tens of millions of viewers via their cell phones. Another example is the Manchester United Football Stadium in the UK. Tens of thousands of fans can access a large range of services and content from their mobile devices, including replays, merchandise and food ordering, and directions to the closest restrooms and vending areas. Mass collaboration moves organizations from a traditional duplex model of communication (one-to-one) to a multiplex mode of communication (one-to-many or even many-to-many).

Wireless Social Networking

As mentioned earlier, wireless is already playing a major role as a communications tool for nonprofits and humanitarian causes. Companies that encourage their employees to engage in activities of social responsibility will benefit from more satisfied and engaged employees. They also will have more networked employees who tap into new markets, geographies, and potential customer populations. Here are some examples of NGO missions that draw on a variety of participants using wireless as a primary connection platform:

- Save the Elephants in Kenya, where wireless is used both to track the location of elephant populations and communicate this information to interested supporters and donors[3]
- Greenpeace in Argentina, which uses text messaging to alert supporters of new actions (like tree plantings and legislative opposition)
- Internet Sexuality Information Services (ISIS), which uses wireless networks to communicate with at-risk populations and community supporters for surveys, educational information, and ongoing counseling

Key Insight

Wireless success factors cut across everything from technology and operating models to organization structure and culture. Organizations must understand where their gaps are to position for success in the Digital Swarm.

Assessing Your Need and Readiness: WiQ

Given the difficulty of predicting how the 4G wireless future or Digital Swarm will change how we live and work, it will be critical for companies to adapt quickly to whatever future emerges. The common wireless success factors or winning attributes just discussed provide an essential foundation to position for success in the Digital Swarm. The level and pervasiveness of these attributes in a given organization is wireless IQ (WiQ). Depending on the industry and specific market environment, organizations may require different levels of WiQ to maximize their overall wireless value-creation opportunity. This need is represented by the following factors:

- **Wireless disruption to markets**—The level of disruption/change that advances in wireless technology, networks, and applications could cause to your markets and customers (new entrants, new products/services, new customer segments)

- **Wireless disruption to business operations**—The level of disruption/change that advances in wireless technology, networks, and applications could cause to your current business operations (productivity, transaction cost, cycle times, footprint)
- **The organization's wireless potential**—The opportunity to leverage wireless to enhance your organization's overall performance (innovation, growth, efficiency)
- **Employee demand**—The percentage of employees demanding greater freedom to conduct all their business activities wirelessly

Based on a recent survey of over 50 top executives across a range of industry sectors and company sizes, the overall gap between the perceived need for WiQ and the organization's actual level of WiQ is significant. Figure 5.2 shows a plot of the average assessment by executives of their organization on each WiQ attribute on a scale from 1 to 7, with 7 being world-class and 1 being nonexistent.

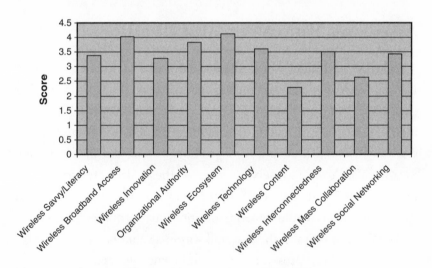

Figure 5.2   WiQ assessment (executive survey results)[4]

In general, executives see their organizations as below average on the majority of WiQ dimensions. Wireless broadband access and wireless ecosystem were the two strongest attributes. They may represent areas where most organizations can build on initiatives that are already under way. Wireless content and wireless mass collaboration were the two weakest attributes. They could represent real blind spots where most organizations need to take significant steps to catch up.

Figure 5.3 shows an assessment by the same executive group of each dimension of WiQ need on a scale from 1 to 7, with 7 being most severe and 1 being insignificant.

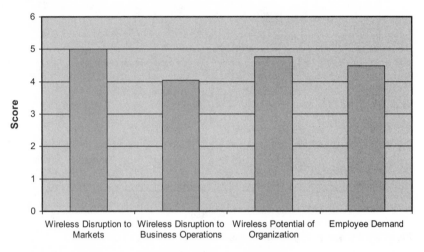

Figure 5.3   WiQ need (executive survey results)[5]

The need for WiQ scored above average on all four dimensions. Wireless disruption to markets and the organization's potential to benefit from wireless were the highest-scoring need areas. This poses a cat-and-mouse-type situation in which wireless-related market disruptions are expected and the company needs to be equipped to take advantage of these to stay competitive. The lowest-scoring need was wireless disruption to business operations. This might have been driven by the view that wireless operates primarily outside the company's walls, which may also be a blind spot for many organizations. Even employee demand scored relatively high. "Consumerized" employees want to dictate what devices and services they have access to at work and home, which puts pressure on companies to change their policies to accommodate these needs.

Executives were also asked to assess the expected pace of progress in wireless that they will need to keep up with. The organizations' overall need, readiness (WiQ), and expected technology progress are shown together in Figure 5.4 on a normalized scale. As you can see, expected progress in wireless developments exceeds current WiQ or wireless readiness by over 25%.

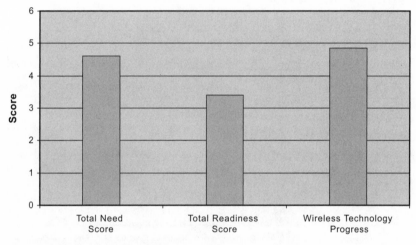

Figure 5.4   Summary of wireless need versus readiness[6]

In other words, a large perceived gap exists between the organizations' current WiQ and what they need to succeed in an unwired future. Appendix A shows the WiQ survey and detailed results. Organizations with a WiQ that exceeds their need are classified as "wireless innovators," and those that have a deficit in WiQ versus their need are classified as "wireless laggards." Based on the executive survey, most organizations fall into the second group.

Key Insight

A significant gap exists in most organizations between their perceived need for wireless IQ and their current WiQ level. This presents a significant opportunity to differentiate for organizations that can overcome the gap.

As companies begin to awaken to the fact that wireless will be a key platform for both value creation and destruction in their industries, a framework like WiQ for assessing organizational capabilities will be fundamental. Industry leaders will need to move quickly beyond basic wireless connectivity to integrate wireless into all activities of their enterprise as well as their organizational culture. But how can an organization use WiQ as a tool to inform future strategy and investments?

A Deeper Look at WiQ

A useful method for assessing the WiQ of your organization and understanding where your gaps may be the greatest is using a spider plot, as shown in Figure 5.5. The outer ring represents the "best in class" or "leading edge" for each dimension. The middle ring represents the target level given the industry you compete in and what will be required for future success. To establish the targets for each WiQ attribute, each organization must not only estimate where the current competition will be, but also consider if a new player could enter with a best-in-class WiQ capability to disrupt the market. An example could be a portable media player company that builds a best-in-class competency in seamless networking. By having a device that can download, refresh, play, and stream content continuously across home, car, office, and remote environments, such a company could easily disrupt the car audio, satellite radio, and home media player markets.

The inner ring represents your current performance on each dimension. When the gaps are identified across the board versus the target levels, the organization can decide which gaps it will expend resources on to close. Some of these may be quick wins and require limited investment, while others may require large investments and significant organizational change. In the figure, the organization has significant gaps on several WiQ attributes, but it may decide to tackle these in stages. For instance, distributed decision-making may require a significant cultural and behavior change in addition to new processes. So this may be put on a longer implementation cycle versus wireless innovation, where a new wireless application development lab or R&D partnerships could be proven out in the near term. These investments may have to be staged to manage overall investment risk and limit the disruption to the organization.

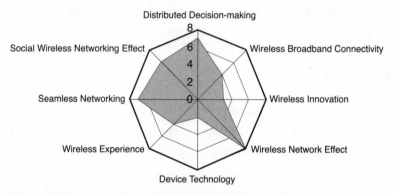

Figure 5.5   "Swarm readiness" spider plot of WiQ gaps

Two of the most significant WiQ parameters (and maybe the most difficult to achieve) are distributed decision-making and wireless networking effect. Looking at just these two key capabilities, organizations can take a quick snapshot of their Swarm readiness, as shown in Figure 5.6.

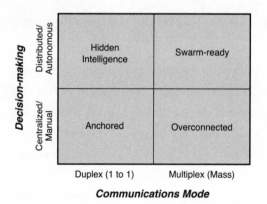

Figure 5.6   Assessing an organization's Swarm readiness

Organizations that use duplex communications and still use manual and centralized decision-making are "anchored" in a model that has little flexibility to take advantage of new wireless changes on the edge. Those that still employ wireless as a duplex communications medium but have distributed organizations have "hidden intelligence" that is not flowing freely across the organization to the right decision-makers. Organizations that can leverage a mass collaboration model for wireless communications across employees, partners, and customers but maintain a hierarchical decision-making structure are over-stimulated and "overconnected." Finally, organizations that can deploy a true wireless ecosystem of interconnected individuals coupled with a distributed and autonomous organization structure will be highly adaptive and "Swarm-ready."

Key Insight

Becoming "Swarm-ready" means letting go of control and allowing key communications to happen well beyond the traditional organizational boundaries. Embracing this concept versus resisting it will be critical to success.

Organizational Implications

Just like any significant change in organizations, to succeed in transforming your WiQ, you must have a shared vision of where you want to go, recognition of the need for change, the capacity to change in the organization, and actionable first steps.[7] The shared vision must be based on a realistic assessment of both future opportunities and current capabilities so that you can select which battles you will fight. Suppose you are publishing company with strong digital content, and you believe that mobile e-readers will become the dominant form of book consumption. You may have a shared vision to become the leader in ubiquitous libraries to allow readers to access any book, anywhere. The key is that your employees buy into this as the right direction for the company. The burning need for change may be to beat your competition to this market opportunity before they stake it out. To create the urgency, you may need to point out past competitive losses or what's at stake if you don't get there first. The capacity for change will depend on what capabilities are needed to achieve the vision. The elements of WiQ that would be needed to support a ubiquitous library are as follows:

- **Wireless broadband**—Employees and customers will need to be connected at high speeds to have low delay in downloading new books.
- **Wireless innovation**—Being able to quickly innovate new applications around wireless books will be key to building a competitive advantage.
- **Device technology**—Creating an ecosystem of capable, connected mobile e-readers will be critical to success, including employee devices.
- **Wireless experience**—Managing the wireless experience will be required to attract and retain customers.
- **Seamless networking**—E-readers will need to work seamlessly across networks to ensure that users can access and interact with books anywhere on demand.
- **Social wireless networking effect** will be essential for sourcing, developing, publishing, and sharing new book content among employees and customers.

The organization must understand the skills, activities, and resources required to "move the needle" in each of these areas to the required level of competency. For example, the publishing company may need to hire several device experts to join its publishing team and adopt a social networking platform to share book content at different stages of development. In addition, cultural barriers to change must be surfaced and addressed before real transformation can take place. Last, actionable first steps or quick wins must be identified to move the organization forward in small steps on what seems like an imposing amount of change. For instance, running a small pilot on two-way interactive books to show user interest could be an achievable near-term step.

You now have a better sense of what capabilities are needed to unlock the power of the Digital Swarm in organizations. The next chapter looks at how you can monitor the wireless sector and your own industry for early signs of future scenarios like Nature Aligns and Killer Bees. It also discusses what developments are happening in different geographies. This will be critical for knowing which of the WiQ attributes you may need to focus on and to identify and execute contingent strategies targeted at specific segments and scenarios.

6

Monitoring and Adapting to Early Signals

"The key is to quickly spot those signals that are relevant and explore them further, filter out the noise, and pursue opportunities ahead of the competition or recognize the early signs of trouble before they escalate into major problems."

—*George Day and Paul Schoemaker*[1]

What do you need to watch related to the Digital Swarm? What really matters? What early signals might you be missing? Many organizations miss the changes at the periphery of their industries because they are so focused on today's performance. As a result, significant value gets created and destroyed as disruption takes place in an established industry sector. As we have discussed in the previous chapters, the Digital Swarm has enormous potential to disrupt traditional markets by changing how employees, customers, and other stakeholders organize, interact, and make decisions. In turn, this will change the way many goods and services are designed, manufactured, tested, distributed, used, and maintained. The companies that see these emerging changes the fastest will be able to adapt their strategies to capture new opportunities by leveraging the Digital Swarm to win in their market.

Figure 6.1 shows how scanning and monitoring are fundamental to creating an effective wireless ecosystem in addition to wireless innovation, rapid customer rollouts, and feedback/learning activities.

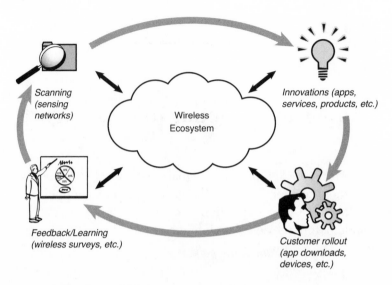

Figure 6.1   Key activities to create a wireless ecosystem

The key to this cycle is the connection between monitoring and experimentation, which really encompasses innovation, rollout, and feedback. Wireless itself offers an incredible platform for learning, because you can quickly pilot new wireless applications via download and then survey customers via text messaging with very little capital commitment. In a highly uncertain market (as is the case with 4G-related products and services), the volatility favors many small bets versus just a few large ones. With small bets, you can learn quickly and then decide to either accelerate, hold, or kill these investments based on how the external environment plays out. The investment can be small relative to the payoff in terms of both market opportunity and information gained. You can also string together a number of bets of increasing size and commitment as the business case becomes more favorable for a given opportunity. Much like financial options, this approach is known as real options or embedded options.[2] The following sidebar describes an example of real options applied to a potential corporate wireless innovation opportunity. When used in conjunction with monitoring, embedded options can be a very powerful tool for managing risk and capturing the upside of opportunities in highly uncertain environments.

Embedded Options in Action

A consumer products company decides to invest in a new wireless product diagnostic capability that relays product information via the Internet using any available wireless network near the consumer's home. The company believes this will cut service and repair costs in half, but it also believes significant risk is involved in achieving this benefit. Here are the top risks the company has identified:

- **Technology**—Enabling the chipset in the product to sense key diagnostics and connect with any available wireless network. This will require an advanced or software-defined radio.

- **Performance**—If the product is kept in a place where wireless access is weak or limited, the wireless diagnostic may not work.

- **User acceptance**—Users may not want a product manufacturer having access to their wireless network without explicit permission. They may also have security features enabled, preventing simple ad hoc access by third parties.

- **Employee adoption**—Employees may resist a technology that potentially displaces their job due to lower demand for human involvement in service and repair.

The investment to roll out this capability to all the company's service and repair units across all products and regions is roughly $2 million. If the new wireless diagnostic solution is successful, the company would save about $1.5 million per year, resulting in a project Net Present Value (NPV) of about $3.3 million. If it fails, the company must write off $2 million. But given the significant uncertainty around the success of such a new technology and business process, the estimated chance of achieving a successful rollout is just 30%, yielding an expected NPV of –$410,000. Figure 6.2 shows the investment and potential outcomes.

One way to effectively manage the risks of this potentially high-risk but high-payoff wireless initiative is to use a phased or embedded options approach consisting of the following phases:

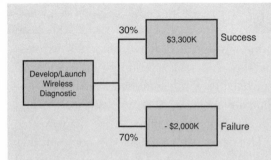

NPV= 30% * ($3,300K) + 70% * (-$2,000K) = -$410K

Figure 6.2   Wireless service and repair investment example: baseline case

1. Perform a study assessing the viability of the technology and a survey of employee acceptance.

2. Pilot and demonstrate the technology with a small service and repair unit for one product line.

3. Roll out the product diagnostic solution for a region or portfolio of products.

4. Perform a full-scale rollout across all regions and products.

For each phase, the required investment and potential outcomes are shown in Figure 6.3.

By taking an embedded options approach, the NPV goes from highly negative to positive by breaking the initiative into stages with updated information before executing the next option. This increases the chance of financial success in the final deployment. As you can see, not only does the embedded options approach give you flexibility in how you execute high-risk initiatives, but this flexibility also translates into real value. For investments related to the highly uncertain Digital Swarm, the embedded options approach can be used as a tool to manage risk as future scenarios unfold. This ensures that your organization captures the full upside of new opportunities without being exposed to a significant downside impact.

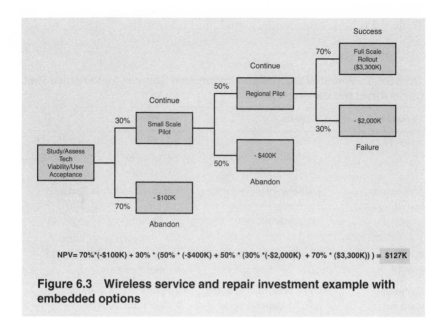

NPV= 70%*(-$100K) + 30% * (50% * (-$400K) + 50% * (30% *(-$2,000K) + 70% * ($3,300K))) = $127K

Figure 6.3 Wireless service and repair investment example with embedded options

To inform an adaptive strategy that maximizes the Digital Swarm opportunity for a given organization, a monitoring and scanning system should be established to pick up and track key signals in the external environment. These signals can be analyzed to determine which future scenario may be emerging for the Digital Swarm. By continually updating assumptions about where the unwired future is headed, the organization can decide when to execute high-payoff opportunities and also mitigate potential threats on the horizon.

Key Insight

Embedded options plus a proactive external monitoring system provide a powerful framework for managing risk for highly uncertain opportunities like the Digital Swarm.

Chapter 3 identified the key variables that could have the biggest impact on scenarios for the unwired future. Now we need to identify signals to monitor that would help project where these variables are headed. In turn, this should help us determine which elements of the two future scenarios (Nature Aligns and Killer Bees) are emerging.

Table 6.1 describes potential signals and information sources for each
of these variables.

**TABLE 6.1   Potential Signals and Information Sources for Variables That
Could Affect the Unwired Future**

Variable	Signals	Sources
Network trust	Statistics on attacks, threats, vulnerabilities, wireless Internet usage	Security agencies, security software companies, wireless network operators
Technology breakthroughs	Technology investment, product launches, patent filings, system/device capabilities	Venture capitalists, tech company R&D reports, USPTO, CTIA
Wireless market growth	Wireless subscribers and usage by geography	Market research, CTIA, ITU, wireless analysts
Strength of economy	GDP, consumer spending, inflation, spending on wireless	Department of Commerce, World Bank, analysts
Killer applications	New wireless application releases, investment in wireless application development, wireless usage by application type	Network operator statistics, CTIA, wireless analysts
Standards alignment	Number of competing standards, number of companies supporting new wireless standards, wireless standard penetration rates	CTIA, ITU, standards organizations, wireless analysts
Low-end disruption	Wireless device cost, wireless service cost, number of new entrants	Network operator pricing, device manufacturer pricing
Wireless social networks	Number of subscribers using wireless social networks	Network usage statistics, wireless and Internet analysts
Seamless mobility	Number of networks that interconnect, wireless connection drops	Wireless standards bodies, network operator call statistics
Embedded sensors	Number of wireless sensors deployed, number of wireless sensor networks	Zigbee alliance, sensor companies
Gen Z dominance	Gen Z wireless usage, number of new applications targeting Gen Z	CTIA, wireless research, social networking sites, blogs

TABLE 6.1 Potential Signals and Information Sources for Variables That Could Affect the Unwired Future

Variable	Signals	Sources
Distributed authority	Average number of layers in corporations	HR or OD organizations and associations
Cognitive devices	Number of "smart" devices on the market with cognitive features, investment in cognitive device technologies	Wireless and tech journals, network provider device catalogs, analysts
Health/environment concerns	Number of medical journal articles/reports connecting wireless and health, lawsuits	Medical journals, media reports, legal proceedings

Many leading indicators or "weak signals" from the Digital Swarm have the potential to emerge and disrupt the market. The risk of monitoring only a few is potentially missing the broader patterns of change. In addition to the variables identified in the scenario exercise, there could be other potentially disruptive areas related to the Digital Swarm that your organization should probe. This will ensure that you are not blindsided by a major shift in the external environment, such as a new technology, business model, or regulatory change. Ironically, it is your organization's extended network enabled by wireless that provides one of the best platforms to scan for weak signals. These networks often extend into customer groups, technology vendors, channel partners, and even financial markets. The following sidebar describes a scanning example for a publishing company and where it should probe for possible wireless disruptions to its business and industry.

Scouting for Signals of Change: Publishing Company Example

Publishers are not always thought of as forward-thinking relative to technology. Yet the publishing industry could be one of the most vulnerable to disruption by the Digital Swarm. Just as the Internet has negatively impacted the circulation of newspapers and books by "democratizing" media, 4G wireless may stretch publishing in an entirely new direction. We already see new business models emerging within the rigid boundaries of present-day wireless systems such as Kindle, which lets you download and read any book via a wireless connection and a device that closely replicates the reading experience. As we move into the Digital Swarm paradigm with immersive user experiences, publishing may take on a completely different meaning. Not only will users be able to read books, they will be able to participate in them via augmented reality (AR). The media and information to create and enhance the experience may be pulled from a variety of sources, not just the content from the publisher. Language and even accent translation would be automatic to accommodate the user's specific profile.

Let's assume you are a large publishing company, PubCo, thinking about how the Digital Swarm might affect your business in the future. You should ask the following questions:

- What new business models may evolve for publishing in the Digital Swarm?

- How will money be made? Will it be from content or services? How will profits be divided?

- How will new content be reviewed and rated?

- How will new writers be identified, and what will they expect?

- How will changes in device technology change the reading experience?

- How will privacy and security threats affect what people are willing to participate in?

- Will the Digital Swarm enable greater collaboration in the development and syndication of content?

- What kind of radical business process changes could be enabled by 4G in the publishing business?

Based on just this set of questions and the range of possible outcomes, a lot of uncertainty exists around how the Digital Swarm could impact PubCo's business in the future. It would be prudent for the company to set up a monitoring system that will pick up new signals and track the development of these potentially disruptive areas. This way, the company can act ahead of the change to not only avoid erosion of its traditional business but also to innovate and create a competitive advantage in the market. An example would be if PubCo picked up a weak signal that a publisher in India had made all of its content available for download and editing by any mobile user for a flat fee service. This includes all multimedia, which could be used for immersion experiences, education and training, and basic consumption as well. This means that formerly copyrighted content can now be altered freely anywhere by any user. This radically different model would mean that the aftermarket for content in "chunks" would be more valuable than the primary market for whole content. As this signal becomes stronger, PubCo may choose to proactively launch its own content aftermarket for wireless users and transition to back-end revenue-sharing deals with writers and artists, anticipating the decline in basic book sales.

Scouting for Signals of Change: Apparel Company Example

Apparel companies are used to looking for the next fad, whether it's the hottest sneaker, most popular shirt color, or coolest brand of jeans. This information mostly comes from hard-core customer research, as in the case of Reebok using "cool hunters" to scout fashion trends in nightclubs and other social hot spots.[3] As wireless technology becomes more integrated with clothing, this on-the-ground intelligence may become critical not just for the apparel companies but also for wireless providers. Today we already have iPods integrated with sneakers and health monitors integrated with watches. So how far could this go as the Digital Swarm hits the market?

Let's assume you are a large apparel company, ApCo, thinking about how the Digital Swarm might affect your business in the future. You should ask the following questions:

- What new business models may evolve for apparel in the Digital Swarm?

- How will money be made? Will it be for clothing, technology, or even services? How will profits be divided?

- Will it be more socially acceptable to have technology hidden or visible in future apparel?

- Who will develop future apparel—technologists or designers?

- How will the price of clothing change, and what will be the resulting benefit to wearers?

- Will the Digital Swarm enable clothing to become "smart" and easily interact with other peripherals and devices?

- What kind of radical business process changes could be enabled by 4G in the apparel business?

Based on just this set of questions and the range of possible outcomes, a lot of uncertainty exists around how the Digital Swarm could impact ApCo's business in the future. As in the PubCo example, the company should set up a monitoring system that will pick up new signals and track the development of these potentially disruptive areas. An example would be if ApCo picked up a weak signal that another clothing manufacturer gives away a free wireless data service if the customer buys one of its "smart shirts." Because the shirt is networked, it can adjust its own cooling or heating features based on picking up the current temperature data. Because the shirt comes with an unlimited data plan, many users buy it as a way to get cheap messaging services. As this signal becomes stronger, ApCo may choose to proactively launch its own smart shirt. It might even develop custom applications that use information from the shirt and other devices to improve convenience for the user. An example would be a body mass index sensor in the shirt that is then tied to dietary recommendations while the user is in the store.

The signals discussed in this chapter are just examples of what an organization or leader may choose to monitor in developing and adapting winning strategies for the Digital Swarm. How you choose to create your own wireless monitoring system depends on several things:

- **Leadership**—Are your leaders willing to challenge their current assumptions and probe the edge of emerging wireless technologies and business models to interpret how they could impact your business? Are they willing to take risks and experiment to exploit new opportunities that future wireless scenarios may present?

- **Process**—Do you have processes that systematically collect and interpret intelligence from employees, partners, customers, and other sources to update your assumptions about the 4G ecosystem and how it may be evolving? Do your processes balance inputs from people within the company and those outside the company who may have more radical or unbiased perspectives?

- **Systems**—Can your information systems support the collection and updating of these signals on the Digital Swarm and get them to the right decision-makers? Are there applications to help visualize the impacts of the Digital Swarm on the organization's current and future actions?

- **Culture**—Does your culture support collaboration and information sharing across organizational boundaries (R&D, marketing, sales, corporate) to see broader patterns of change in the wireless arena? Are incentives in place to facilitate and sustain this?

Without these fundamentals in place, it will be difficult to develop an active monitoring and scanning system for 4G and the broader Digital Swarm and also to innovate based on new signals of change.

Key Insight

Leadership, processes, systems, and culture must all be aligned for you to effectively sense and adapt to new signals from the Digital Swarm and create new innovation opportunities for the organization.

The next chapter describes some of the innovation opportunities that could emerge from companies exploiting the Digital Swarm to their advantage.

7

Killer Swarm Apps

> "Guessing what the pitcher is going to throw is eighty percent of being a successful hitter. The other twenty percent is just execution."
>
> —*Hank Aaron*

We know the Digital Swarm will surprise us with some curveballs. But we also need to take enough swings to get a hit or even a home run. So what are some of the specific innovation opportunities that may be enabled by the Digital Swarm where your organization can take its swings or place smart bets? This chapter plants some seeds for early adopters by framing several specific innovation opportunities, or Killer Swarm Apps. The applications that will be discussed are

- Foresight for Drivers
- Context-Aware Retailing
- Organizational Behavior Tracking
- Pervasive Healthcare

The following sections discuss the current challenge, the Killer Swarm App, and the resulting business impact for each of these potential innovations.

Foresight for Drivers

The Challenge

An enormous number of people drive to work each day, including 90% of workers in the United States. Over 80% of goods are moved by truck in the United States. Transportation accounts for roughly 30% of overall energy consumption and 33% of greenhouse gas (GHG) emissions in the United States.[1] As the populations in emerging markets grow and improve their standards of living, this problem could become a global crisis for the environment. Aside from the fact that public transportation needs to become more efficient, especially in the United States, automobile traffic is highly inefficient, with drivers spending 62 hours per year on average in congestion. This results in not only additional fuel and GHG emissions, but also $100 billion in lost productivity and overall aggravation.[2] Given that we will likely rely on automobiles for the next several decades, how can we dramatically improve the system's overall efficiency by leveraging the Digital Swarm?

Killer Swarm App

Bringing together several features of 4G—seamless wireless broadband, mesh networking, location-based services, and cognitive devices—a new traffic system providing real-time situational awareness and decision-making for drivers could be developed. The system would have cars relay key situational information via an ad hoc mesh network to a central database and processing center. This would, in turn, provide an updated "macro" situation map for all users. This map could then be processed locally by the users' cognitive devices to make an optimal decision on their routing. Figure 7.1 shows the Foresight for Drivers solution.

With each automobile acting as a sensor and node in the network, expensive fixed infrastructure could be minimized or even eliminated. Devices could choose the best network alternative (3G, WiMAX, WiFi, Bluetooth) based on the proximity of other cars

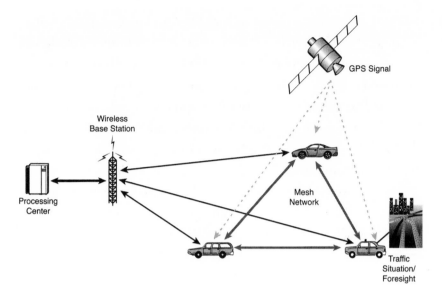

Figure 7.1   Foresight for Drivers solution

(nodes) and the amount of information to relay. Because the computations could be complex, cognitive devices could choose to offload some of the computations to the central processing center or even grid computing resources available via one of their wireless networks. The end result is greater foresight for drivers, allowing for better routing decisions and significantly reduced congestion on the roads.

Business Impact

The business impact of the Foresight for Drivers solution comes in two forms. One is the impact on the road transportation element of every business, whether it is employees commuting or trucks transporting goods. In this category, the reduction in energy consumption and environmental footprint could be enormous. Companies that can equip their vehicles with devices and sensors that can use this network put themselves at a significant advantage. This could even evolve into using the rich data from this network to alter operating times and staffing for the business to maximize the gains in productivity and the reduction in energy and environmental penalties. On the business model side, it is not clear that one player has the scale to roll out this type of system, other than regional and federal governments. It would also take a major change in traditional business models to field this type of solution. Technology players like IBM, Nokia, and Cisco would need to become service providers to make this work and may need to support a variety of equipment outside of their own. Network operators like Verizon, Vodafone, and NTT DoCoMo would need to support the use of mesh networking among different users that they do not earn revenue on today. Application providers like Microsoft, Google, and Navteq would need to be able to tap into user-based sensor information and operate a commercial wireless network, which they do not do today. The question is, will new players emerge at the local or national level to take on this space? Or will one of these players transform its business model to provide this type of valuable service? This area certainly demands further monitoring!

Context-Aware Retailing

The Challenge

Today's shopping experience is far from optimal. Although Internet shopping offers speed, convenience, and the ability to quickly compare prices, it lacks the personal touch, immediacy, and interactive experience of physical stores. However, brick-and-mortar shopping also has its limitations, such as wasted time and fuel, limited ability to compare products and prices across stores, and limited "memory" of your personal preferences. You need to "educate" the salesperson each time you come into the store, or find things yourself. Even on the Internet, current "profiling" engines are weak at best and cannot account for your historic activity across many different e-commerce destinations. Certainly, neither experience is optimal. In addition, the retail experience of driving from store to store, roaming through a shopping mall, or searching for an item in an unfamiliar area (like when you are on vacation) can be one of the most frustrating experiences in everyday life.

Killer Swarm App

Context-Aware Retailing will leverage 4G technologies to give shoppers the convenience of e-commerce coupled with the intimacy of physical stores tailored to their specific needs. The solution leverages location-based services, seamless networking, broadband wireless, and cognitive devices along with social networking to create a full-spectrum, truly personalized shopping experience.

This solution, shown in Figure 7.2, consists of mesh networks at the retail store and mall level. Consumer smartphones, shopping carts, and product displays are interconnected to support direct communications. They also can access a broader relay network through a local wireless access point. Products utilize two-way smart tags to support dynamic pricing accessible by the consumer and store at any time. Consumers can quickly compare product info and pricing to any comparable product in the local region based on their known location from GPS. They also can view interactive product videos and demos to further research their decision in real time. While this may not be necessary for a loaf of bread, it certainly would be appropriate for a plasma TV! As an additional benefit, users will be prompted with personalized product offers and information as they approach different areas of the store or mall, because their location and shopping preference profiles are known.

As the consumers go mobile (walking, driving, riding), they will be prompted with both Internet and physical store retail options based on their specific profile and context. For example, suppose your cognitive device knows that you have been shopping for golf clubs over the last week but have not made a purchase yet. It may prompt you with golf store options and products closely matched to what you have looked at previously. It might even suggest demo and fitting centers close to where you are at the time. If it knows you are away on business or vacation, it may suggest golf club rental options that are very close to the clubs you are interested in. Of course,

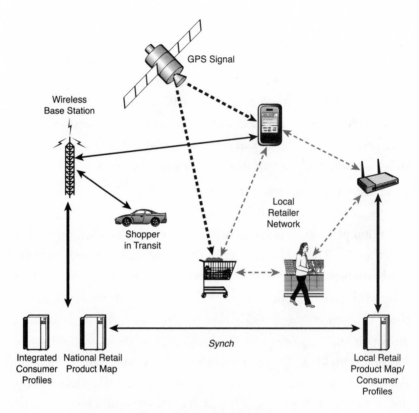

Figure 7.2   Context-Aware Retailing solution

pricing and product comparisons would be fully available, as would the option to purchase and ship online. This would also include the ability to quickly consult social networks for recommended products and opinions. In the most proactive form, Context-Aware Retailing will allow the integration of many lifestyle facets. This might include knowing that a consumer has recently been diagnosed with diabetes and making sure that the system recommends only sugar-free candy. It also could include alerting the consumer to potentially harmful products as she approaches them in the supermarket. The potential to enhance today's shopping experience with 4G is enormous.

Business Impact

The business impact of Context-Aware Retailing on current players and markets could be significant. A more efficient shopping experience will have a lot of positive effects for society in terms of reduced environmental footprint and more free time for other activities (unless your hobby is shopping!). When the location dimension is added, coupled with true decisioning capability based on user preferences, the user becomes much more in control of the retail experience. Retailers will need to operate in real time to keep pace with the changing needs and situations of each consumer. For instance, it would be wasted effort to promote winter clothes knowing that the consumer is about to vacation on a tropical island. Or if the consumer is in the midst of a two-day bike trip and traveling light, he might be willing to pay a premium for athletic wear and nutritional foods that fit his needs. This approach will change how retailers do business. It will favor retailers that invest in predictive analytics and wireless ecosystems around their stores and supply chain. Without smart tags on products and location-aware displays in stores, retailers will miss the opportunity to drive a highly interactive and "sticky" in-store experience for consumers. The big question is, who will manage the overall system and national product database? There are many comparison engines on the web today, but they are certainly not complete with respect to physical retail store products and prices. Also, who will manage the consumer profile information given the critical need for security and privacy? In both cases, the large Internet portals and e-commerce players are certainly in a strong position, but so are the retailers and wireless providers. The consumers may even take more control and form their own buying consortiums to manage this via social networks. This is another area that will need to be monitored closely.

How a Wireless App Is Born

Wireless devices are very different animals than typical PCs in that most of them have a small screen, limited keypad, and no mouse or pointing device. They also may vary widely in features and functions such as voice commands, location information, screen resolution, processing power, and operating system. (Unlike the PC market with Microsoft, no one company has more than 30% of the market.) As a result, developing applications that run on a variety of devices can be challenging.

One of the significant choices is between a "thick" client application, where most of the work is done on the device, and a "thin" client application, where most of the work is done on a remote server. Thick clients typically are better for smartphones or PDAs with greater processing power, memory, screen size, and navigation features. The choices for application development environment include Windows Mobile, Java ME (Mobile Environment), Symbian, Palm, and others. Customer relationship management (CRM) would be a good candidate for a thick client application. Thin clients utilize the browser and require a mobile web connection with sufficient bandwidth. The choice of development environment for thin clients includes Wireless Application Protocol (WAP), HTML (hypertext markup language), and Web Services. Thin clients are ideal for simple tasks that do not require a lot of data or processing.

If your organization decides to develop a new wireless application, here are several key steps to consider:

1. Define the business process flow that must be supported.

2. Define the wireless application requirements to deliver this process.

3. Develop a functional requirements specification, including use cases.

4. Define the data required to support the application.

5. Develop screen mock-ups for the target mobile devices.

6. Develop the application flow (access and ordering of different screens).

7. Select the application architecture that best meets the requirements.

With the emergence of Software Development Kits (SDKs) for the iPhone and BlackBerry, as well as the open Application Programming Interface (API) for Google's Android mobile operating system, wireless applications may be developed by a range of companies and individuals. Mobile application servers are also beginning to appear that will allow single applications to run on several different operating systems analogous to the enterprise IT server world. This innovation ecosystem will continue to grow with the emergence of 4G cognitive devices that incorporate contextual information and that can access almost any network.

Organizational Behavior Tracking

The Challenge

Companies have a limited ability to track the effectiveness of new initiatives or organizational changes in the workplace. This could include new business or operational strategies, process changes, or changes in personnel. Most of this information typically is shielded by organizational layers. These layers require that the performance of individuals and their interaction with others be reported through their line manager and then rolled up for reporting at higher levels. By the time this gets to senior executives, it is too late to make adjustments at the corporate or business unit level to increase the chance of success.

Killer Swarm App

By using the location-aware and mesh networking features of 4G along with behavioral data mining, organizational behavior could be tracked more effectively to inform more proactive decisions when rolling out new initiatives or changes. The Organizational Behavior Tracking solution has several key elements:

- GPS-based location awareness to track the movement of personnel and teams throughout the day
- Mesh networking to facilitate rapid peer-to-peer communication, information sharing, and collaboration

- Behavioral data mining to track the patterns of interaction and collaboration in terms of both frequency and intensity

The overall solution is shown in Figure 7.3.

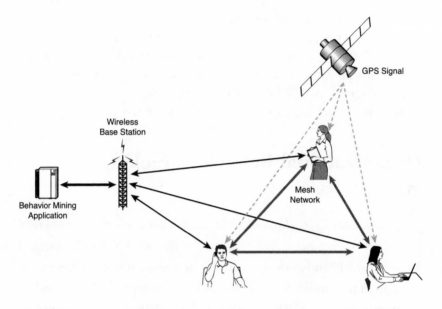

Figure 7.3   Organizational Behavior Tracking solution

This approach allows executives to create a high-level map showing the hot spots of both success and inactivity in rolling out new initiatives based on Social Network Analysis (SNA). An example is a company that has a strategy to target small businesses as a new customer segment for its products and that creates a sales and marketing campaign around this initiative. Organizational Behavior Tracking could be used to monitor if the sales force is actually making substantial visits to small-business locations and if they are doing this in teams or alone. It also could tell you to what extent the small-business sales leaders are interacting with other folks on the sales and marketing teams to launch this key initiative. You could also plot a geographic map to see the relative penetration of small-business sales interactions in the target region.

Business Impact

The impact of Organizational Behavior Tracking on businesses could be significant. Two fundamental shifts could occur as part of this new approach. One is that employees become comfortable with transparency in exchange for achieving better overall organizational performance. Given that we have talked about how the Gen Z'ers are very comfortable sharing profile information about themselves with others if they think it will create some higher-level benefit, this shift may already be happening. However, for the more established workforce, finding ways to provide this functionality while protecting their privacy will be key. (For instance, knowing when and where a person goes to the doctor or to her kid's sporting event may be out of bounds.) With increased teleworking and work-life convergence, this presents significant challenges. But the payoff could be a much more efficient workforce with the ability to adjust processes and eliminate barriers to progress and even poor performers on a continual basis. In theory, this will keep your best performers happy and could create a competitive advantage for the company. The second big shift is in how you do business. With this type of capability in place, new initiatives could be piloted much more quickly to determine whether they will work. Dysfunctional parts of the organization can be quickly spotted and dealt with. Companies that adopt this strategy can become much more experimental and innovative. The key questions are, who will run the system? The company or an outside service provider? Will it be in the form of software or services or both? Will companies use this to create a competitive advantage or just to keep pace with efficiency? Finally, what are the legal liabilities of companies that choose to adopt this approach? Will it become like e-discovery, where employee hard drives and mobile devices are open targets for data mining? Organizational Behavior Tracking strikes at the heart of the privacy-versus-benefits trade-off and will need to be watched closely as a disruptive 4G application.

Pervasive Healthcare

The Challenge

Today, healthcare delivery is highly inefficient. Many patients have to travel significant distances to points of care just to be evaluated or diagnosed for something routine. This also applies to patients who require continuous monitoring and either the patient or doctor must travel for a live evaluation. In many cases, patients do not make the trip when they have symptoms or early warning signs of illness because they underestimate their condition or need to see a doctor. This can result in more severe illness or death if treatment does not happen in time. Last, chronic disease is a major contributor to healthcare costs. Over 7 million Americans have diabetes, and cardiovascular disease and stroke alone resulted in $450 billion in U.S. healthcare costs in 2008.[3] Proactive monitoring could significantly reduce healthcare costs, especially hospitalization, by preventing acute conditions from occurring. How could the current model of monitoring and managing chronic disease be dramatically improved using the Digital Swarm?

Killer Swarm App

Patients would wear a monitoring device (watch, ankle bracelet, necklace, ring) that has built-in biosensors (blood pressure, glucose, heart rate) and a wireless transmitter that can relay information to the patient's mobile device. In addition, implanted devices such as pacemakers, neuro-stimulators, and artificial joints would relay their telemetry to the wearable sensor or mobile device. The connections between sensors, devices, and the handset can all be short-range wireless standards such as Bluetooth or Zigbee. Or a direct long-range connection could be used, such as WiMAX or LTE. Figure 7.4 shows the Pervasive Healthcare solution.

This approach would give doctors near-real-time data on the patient's condition both to detect early signs of a change in the

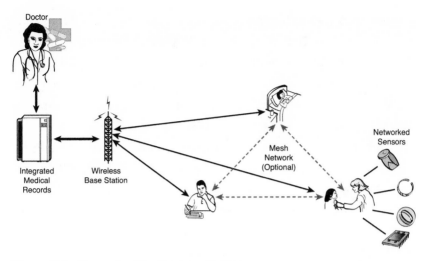

Figure 7.4 Pervasive Healthcare solution

person's condition and to determine the appropriate treatment. This could even be used for healthy patients to determine when they are at risk of possible illness. The last element in the Pervasive Healthcare solution is the ability to remotely diagnose and counsel patients via their mobile device. With secure high-definition videoconferencing capability enabled by 4G, doctors could view any part of a patient's body, such as limbs, ears, or throat, without requiring a visit. Coupled with the monitoring data already being provided, this could significantly reduce healthcare costs, patient travel time, and energy consumption. It could also be invaluable for responding to emergency situations in remote environments or with patients in transit, where the doctor cannot physically get to the patient.

Business Impact

The business impact of the Pervasive Healthcare solution could be enormous. Healthcare costs are expected to exceed $4 trillion, or 20% of U.S. GDP, by 2020.[4] Almost half of this is related to chronic disease that could be better managed through preventive care and monitoring. Hospitalization is roughly one third of overall healthcare costs, so reducing this by even a small percentage through proactive care could be enormous for businesses and the economy. Also, the environmental footprint of hospitals, clinics, doctors' offices, and patient transportation is significant and could be greatly reduced through a Pervasive Healthcare solution. This will disrupt the current healthcare services market by shifting to a patient-centric model in which wireless network providers and monitoring service companies provide significant value for patients and doctors. Meanwhile, hospitals and clinics may become less critical and will need to search for new revenue streams if in-patient services decline. It will be less important for doctors to be part of practices and more important that they have a strong track record of accurate diagnosis and healthy patients, whether they are in Baltimore or Bangalore. The question is, who will manage the overall Pervasive Healthcare service, and who will control the patient data collected—healthcare providers, wireless operators, insurance companies, device companies, or application vendors? The opportunity is wide open.

Getting the Right DNA

Whichever combination of technologies and applications perseveres as part of 4G, it will survive because the ecosystem of devices, networks, and applications (DNA) provides mutual benefit and supports a sustainable growth model. This is illustrated in Figure 7.5.

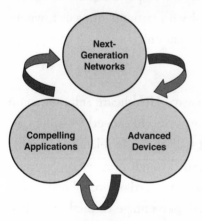

Figure 7.5   Wireless device, network, and application ecosystem

The traditional view has always been "If you build it, they will come." This means that device vendors and application developers will innovate compelling new offerings if a next-generation network exists. However, what we have seen with disruptive technologies and platforms like file sharing, social networking, and even Internet-based voice like Skype is that putting open devices and networks (like the Internet or mash-ups) in the hands of users spurs disruptive innovation. This drives new applications that the networks must now accommodate to be relevant. This alternative model is shown in Figure 7.6.

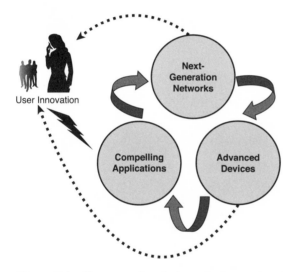

Figure 7.6   User-centric wireless device, network, and application ecosystem

This user-centric model represents the largest, most transformational difference in 4G networks from the networks of today and what preceded them.

Key Insight

Killer Swarm Apps will appear in virtually every industry. Capturing these opportunities with minimal risk will require an iterative approach that refines each application based on user feedback.

8

Swarm Leadership

"Innovation distinguishes between a leader and a follower."
—*Steve Jobs*

We have taken a journey from the recent evolution of wireless as a powerful new communications capability to the not-too-distant future. There, wireless becomes an enabler for social interaction, innovation, and the creation and disruption of business models and markets. This final chapter summarizes the "stuff that matters" from this book and proposes a potential leadership agenda to win in the Digital Swarm.

Knowing what's important and leading the change (as opposed to having the change impact you) applies to all levels of action, whether it's your industry, company, career, or personal life. Whether you are an executive, manager, employee, student, or just a curious reader, 4G will affect your life in a transformative way. Here are the key points we have covered in our journey:

- **Cellular systems were nascent for decades,** restrained by a lack of vision on the part of monopolistic players and the government, with little regard for the market potential of wireless communications. No one estimated how big wireless would become, now with nearly 4 billion users. It would not be difficult to imagine another big "surprise" on the horizon in wireless.
- **3G has not provided the "bang for the buck" after much fanfare.** The needs of users have grown beyond the incremental

improvements that 3G provides. As a result, other technologies (HSPA, Next-Gen WiFi, and WiMax) are filling the gap.

- **4G has no commonly accepted standard or definition.** There are goals like 1Gbps and seamless connectivity, as well as a collection of leading-edge technologies such as cognitive radio, mesh networks, and sensor networks. Standards like LTE and WiMax have labeled themselves 4G networks, but the reality is that there is still a huge amount of uncertainty around what 4G will become.

- **The Digital Swarm is not just about technology.** Like many other disruptive technologies, the confluence of social, economic, and political drivers leads to a "tipping point" where the technology takes off. For the Digital Swarm, these drivers include low-end disruptions, empowered groups, Gen Z users, bioconvergence, contextual intelligence, work-life convergence, embedded objects, IP regimes, and atomized authority.

- **Several frameworks are required to understand how the Digital Swarm may evolve in the future.** Given the significant uncertainty and complexity in projecting the unwired future, systems thinking and scenario planning are used to understand and bound the interactions and resulting market outcomes that may take place.

- **The unwired future could play out across a range of scenarios,** with possibilities including a cooperative, high-trust future scenario (Nature Aligns) or a fractured, insecure wireless future scenario (Killer Bees). This depends on the interactions of several key drivers, such as network security, collaboration, and technology ownership.

- **Organizations must identify success strategies that work across a range of unwired future scenarios.** While organizations should have contingent strategies that will pay off in specific future scenarios or market segments, they should balance these with core success strategies that pay off across most scenarios and market segments.

- **An executive survey has identified WiQ, a set of common organizational characteristics for success in the unwired future.** WiQ covers wireless savvy and literacy, wireless broadband access, wireless innovation, organizational authority, wireless ecosystem, wireless technology, wireless content, wireless interconnectedness, wireless mass collaboration, and wireless social networking.

- **Companies must establish a wireless ecosystem that facilitates the innovation of new products, services, and business models.** The ecosystem should utilize the organization's extended networks of employees, partners, and customers to scan for new signals, innovate and launch new offerings, and collect feedback and learning from the market.

- **"Killer Swarm Apps" will soon appear, disrupting current markets and creating new ones by leveraging 4G wireless.** Foresight for drivers, context-aware retailing, organizational behavior tracking, and pervasive healthcare are just a few examples of where these Killer Swarm Apps could happen.

Organizations should consider these takeaways as input for developing their own Digital Swarm strategy. However, this will take significant leadership, because the unwired future is very much still emerging. The tyranny of near-term priorities and quarterly business performance tends to drain many of the resources and much of the leadership attention from longer-term market opportunities like the Digital Swarm. Innovative companies will find a way to do both by finding "quick wins," deploying wireless applications within their current operations and placing longer-term bets to win in their respective markets by leveraging 4G.

The 4G Organization

As opposed to the "faster car" model of today's 3G networks, 4G redesigns the car to become part of an interconnected system of cars much more capable than any one car on the highway. It is this constant "interconnectedness" that makes the 4G organization so much different than even the "best in class" 3G organizations of today. 4G organization employees may find themselves making informed decisions and sharing content and applications in real time with both employees and users of other social networks anywhere, anytime. The "anywhere" access is delivered via a number of interconnected networks at the micro and macro level. This will be transparent to the users as their devices negotiate the necessary communication paths based on their requirements and company policies/agreements.

The behaviors you may expect to see in a leading-edge 4G wireless organization are as follows:

- A wireless-savvy workforce that uses wireless as its primary means of communicating for all business and personal activities
- The ability for employees' devices to make decisions about what wireless network to use based on location and context anywhere in the world
- Continuous sharing of key information and content to inform better decisions for all employees in any location (mobile or fixed)
- Using the ideal communications medium for each unique interaction, including text, voice, video, email, and other forms
- Having all critical enterprise applications accessible by mobile employees using any approved device
- Continuous refresh of applications and security settings via software downloads to employee mobile devices
- Wireless used as a collaboration and innovation platform by employees, partners, and customers, with "immersive" wireless applications to drive this
- Having a simple development model so that any employee or partner can easily develop and publish a new wireless application
- Having a culture that embraces the power of a highly distributed workforce and that empowers mobile employees to make key decisions and innovate for the business
- Enterprise agreements with a variety of wireless network providers, as well as infrastructure that supports a wide range of 4G wireless communication options

Considering these characteristics, it is easy to see how dramatically different the 4G organization is from today's 3G organization. Table 8.1 summarizes these differences.

TABLE 8.1   3G Versus 4G Wireless Organizations

Attribute	3G Organization	4G Organization
Wireless access	Limited to 3G coverage and WiFi hotspots	Ubiquitous using micro and macro networks
Connection speeds	Slightly less than home broadband speeds	Better than home broadband speeds
Devices	Smartphones and laptops	Cognitive devices with software updates
Organization authority	Centrally controlled	Highly distributed
Wireless enterprise applications	Partial mobile access	Full mobile access plus personalized applications
Knowledge sharing	Centrally accessed	Both central and peer-to-peer access
Security	Controlled at the enterprise level	Controlled at the user level
Interconnected devices	Limited connections via Bluetooth	Full ecosystem of interconnected "things"
Wireless customer interaction	Basic Web site access and mobile marketing	Real-time behavior tracking and interactions

The wireless revolution and enabling technologies in 4G wireless lay the foundation for this new highly distributed, interconnected Digital Swarm organizational paradigm. Because we are in the early stages of 4G technology, very few organizations emulate this paradigm. The U.S. Army is among the few pioneers that exhibit Digital Swarm characteristics—out of necessity, to cope with a highly irregular, constantly changing battlefield environment. Other early adopters of 4G include nonprofits like the UN and the Obama Campaign, which use Digital Swarm approaches to direct support and resources. Companies like FedEx and UPS use Digital Swarm approaches to create a truly agile supply chain, with humans and machines constantly interacting to provide real-time sensing and adjustments.

Figure 8.1 shows the competitive leverage that companies will achieve by changing the wireless paradigm within their organizations from "connectivity" to "seamless experience" to a true "ecosystem."

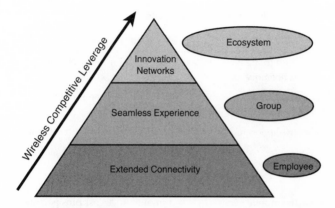

Figure 8.1   The three layers of wireless competitive leverage

Most organizations today live at the first layer, Extended Connectivity, employing wireless as another form of connectivity or communications with primarily one-to-one (duplex) communications. The impact or benefit is essentially achieved at the level of the employee and his individual productivity.

The second layer, Seamless Experience, begins to connect groups and communities of people via wireless around common interests. It enables gains in intelligence and decision-making at the group level.

The third layer, Innovation Networks, creates a broad wireless ecosystem that extends well beyond the organization. It allows information, ideas, resources, and even talent to be sourced from virtually anywhere within this loosely connected system. The competitive leverage gained by your organization moving up to the higher layers can be significant, both in terms of the speed and market impact of new wireless innovations.

Like birds, insects, and fish in nature's ecosystem, swarming will become a common strategy for successful organizations. It will mean changing your leadership model from command and control to adapt and innovate. Hopefully this book has helped you better prepare to create your own Digital Swarm and organize for success in the unwired future.

A

Taking the WiQ Survey

This appendix provides a basic template for taking the WiQ survey for your own organization. It is recommended that you take this across several business units, functional areas, and management levels of the organization and compare the results. It may also be useful to sample results from different demographic groups of employees (young versus old, international versus U.S.-based, and so on). Rate each parameter on a scale from 1 to 7, with 1 being very low/minimal, 4 being moderate, and 7 being very high/pervasive.

Need

Category	Dimension	Rating (1 to 7)
Wireless disruption to markets	The level of disruption/change that advances in wireless technology, networks, and applications could cause to your markets and customers (new entrants, new products/services, new customer segments, and so on)	
Wireless disruption to business operations	The level of disruption/change that advances in wireless technology, networks, and applications could cause to your current business operations (productivity, transaction cost, cycle times, footprint, and so on)	
Wireless potential of the organization	Opportunity to leverage wireless to enhance your organization's overall performance (innovation, growth, and efficiency)	

Need

Category	Dimension	Rating (1 to 7)
Employee demand	The percentage of employees demanding greater freedom to conduct all their business activities wirelessly	
Total Need Score		

Readiness

Category	Dimension	Rating (1 to 7)
Wireless savvy/literacy	The percentage of employees who own latest-generation (3G) wireless devices and subscribe to latest-generation (3G) wireless services	
Wireless broadband access	The penetration of wireless broadband among employees for accessing work applications	
Wireless innovation	The percentage of new products and services that leverage wireless as an enabler or delivery medium	
Organizational authority	The extent to which decision-making authority in the organization is distributed (peer-to-peer) versus centralized (hierarchical)	
Wireless ecosystem	The overall percentage of employees, customers, partners, and vendors who actively connect, communicate, and interact with each other through a wireless network	
Wireless technology	The rate at which wireless technology and applications are updated/refreshed with the latest versions	
Wireless content	The percentage of your organization's content that is geared toward an immersive wireless experience	

Readiness

Category	Dimension	Rating (1 to 7)
Wireless interconnectedness	The level of seamless interconnectivity between your wireless users and your organization's other networks	
Wireless mass collaboration	The extent to which the organization uses text messaging, IM, blogs, and wikis accessed via wireless handhelds to communicate and organize initiatives	
Wireless social networking	The extent to which your employees use wireless for social networking to accomplish higher-level goals beyond just work (relationship building, charity, entertainment, and so on)	
Total Readiness Score		

Based on a survey of over 50 executives, the majority of companies have a wireless readiness score that is less than their wireless need score. (They are wireless laggards.) Only 20% had a wireless readiness score that exceeded their need score. (They are wireless innovators.) Figure A.1 plots the executive survey results. If you find that your scores for wireless need and readiness put you in the laggard category, the next step is to understand which elements in each area (need and readiness) are driving the gap. For instance, in the readiness category, if you scored extremely low on wireless content or wireless social networking, you may want to try a pilot in these areas to explore different applications to determine the most appropriate solution for your organization. In the need category, if you scored high on employee demand, you may want to quickly get a handle on what wireless devices and applications your employees are seeking that you may currently not be supporting and evaluate or pilot these in the near term.

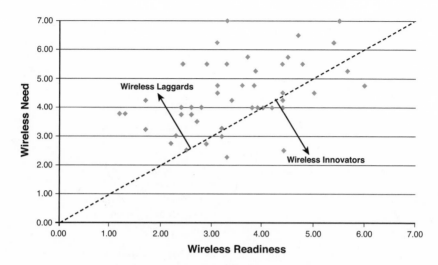

Figure A.1   Wireless need versus wireless readiness

As the Digital Swarm hits the market with the advent of 4G technologies, companies need to be ready to innovate rapidly to gain an advantage. You must address your major gaps now to be positioned for success in the unwired future. The WiQ survey is a good starting point to find out where your organization should focus to gain the most improvement and close the gap.

B

Wireless 101: Inside the Technology

Cellular Communications Basics

The cellular concept is based on three key principles:

- **Frequency reuse**—In cellular systems, communication frequencies can be reused across a group of hexagon-shaped cells, as shown in Figure B.1, each with its own cell tower. This allows operators to maximize the number of users they can support with a given set of frequencies (sometimes called *spectrum*). They typically license this spectrum from a regulatory authority like the FCC unless it is *unlicensed*, where any operator can use it without a fee, as in the case of WiFi.

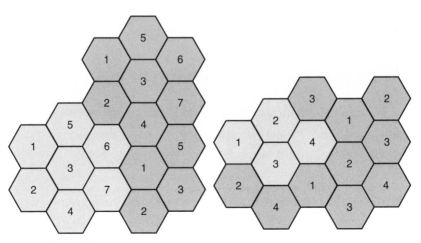

Figure B.1   Cellular frequency reuse patterns

- **Handoffs**—When mobile users move from cell to cell, the cellular network performs a *handoff*, switching the user to a new frequency before entering the new cell to avoid dropping the call. The network can determine when the user is crossing into a new cell by the strength of the signal received by the mobile user's handset from each cell tower.

- **Adding capacity**—When a network needs to support more users in a given location, cells can be divided into smaller cells with lower-power base stations to minimize the interference, as shown in Figure B.2. Because the equipment for a cellular station can cost several hundred thousand to millions of dollars, network operators typically wait until they are maxed out on the number of users they can support before adding another tower and associated equipment.

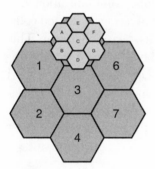

Figure B.2   Dividing a cell for more capacity

What Is Wireless Spectrum?

Wireless spectrum is a portion of the naturally occurring electromagnetic (EM) spectrum that has properties that are conducive to wireless communications among fixed and mobile handheld devices.

Figure B.3 shows this entire EM spectrum and what types of products operate in different bands. Mobile wireless systems tend to operate in the very small slice from 700MHz to 3,000MHz due to the unique properties of transmissions at these frequencies. Frequencies below this band propagate for much longer distances, causing issues for cellular frequency reuse. Also, the size of radio components like antennas grows inversely with respect to the frequency. So handset antennas would become inconveniently bulky at lower frequencies. At frequencies above 3,000MHz, the transmission or *free space* losses become much higher, requiring high power and more costly transmitters in the handsets to overcome this. At even higher frequencies, where fixed wireless systems and satellites (like DirecTV) sometimes operate, the losses become even greater because moisture in the atmosphere starts to affect the signal. (This is why satellite signals sometimes go out during rain or ice storms.)

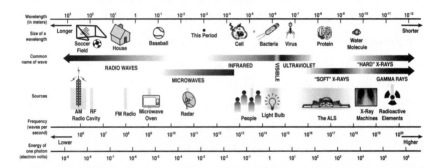

Figure B.3   Applications in different parts of the electromagnetic spectrum (Source: United States Government, National Aeronautics and Space Administration)

As a result, the spectrum most suitable for wireless is viewed as a scarce resource, like real estate in Manhattan or London. It commands a high premium when sold or auctioned off by government regulatory bodies.

What Is Digital?

Digital transmission converts an analog communications stream like your voice, a TV show, or song into a series of 1s and 0s. This is done by sampling the analog signal at regular intervals, at a rate faster than the signal itself is changing (referred to as the Nyquist frequency). The level of each sample is then converted into binary form. (Every number can be written as 1s or 0s in Base 2.) For example, the number 14 would be translated into 1110 in binary form. After all the samples are in binary form, they are assembled into a stream. Additional bits are added as headers, breaks, and codes for checking errors, verifying the integrity of the information, and security protection.

To transmit this binary stream through the air via a wireless signal, a process called modulation is used. Modulation impresses information onto another signal—a wireless signal in this case. Three basic types of modulation can be used: frequency modulation (FM), amplitude modulation (AM), and phase modulation (PM), and combinations of all three. Think of a flashlight being turned on and off at a controlled rate, with the intensity of the light changing at each interval. Frequency modulation is like increasing the rate to transmit a 1 and decreasing the rate to transmit a 0. Amplitude modulation is like setting the light's intensity to high to transmit a 1 and to low to transmit a 0. Phase modulation is like shifting the starting time of the light's on-off cycle by half the cycle time to transmit a 1 and not shifting at all to transmit a 0.

After the bit stream is modulated onto a wireless signal, the receiver at the other end must be able to *demodulate* and *decode* the bit stream using the reverse process of the transmission process just described. This is illustrated in Figure B.4. In addition, the receiver also has knowledge of the *codes*, or additional bits used to fully translate the message from a binary stream into the final application (text, video, audio) and check for errors or tampering.

What Is the Difference Between GSM, CDMA, and TDMA?

The communication streams of several users can be combined over a single communications link in several ways. These are called

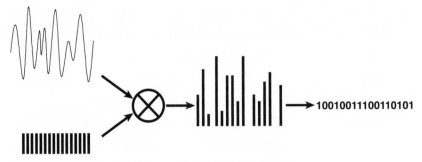

Figure B.4   Demodulation of a digital transmission

access methods. Aside from spatial reuse, discussed as the basic premise of cellular systems, the three primary access methods are Frequency Division Multiple Access (FDMA), Time Division Multiple Access (TDMA), and Code Division Multiple Access (CDMA).

FDMA, used in 1G analog systems, divides the allocated frequency spectrum into several different frequency slots, or *channels*, with a *guard band* in between to limit interference between adjacent channels. FDMA is a fairly simple scheme in that when the transmitter and receiver are assigned to a channel, it does not change (unless it was reassigned when moving into a new cell). This type of frequency division is also used in many telecommunications systems, such as cable and broadcast TV.

TDMA divides the allocated spectrum into time slots. All users transmit on the same frequency, but they are synchronized to transmit or "burst" at different time slots, with small guard time slots in between to limit interference. TDMA is more efficient in terms of data transmitted per a given frequency in terms of bits per Hz than FDMA, but it also requires more sophisticated equipment to ensure that handsets access the appropriate time slot. TDMA may be used in combination with FDMA. The allocated frequency is divided into separate frequencies using FDMA, and then each of these channels is shared among multiple users via TDMA. This is the case in GSM, where the allocated band is divided into 124 channels using FDMA, and each of these channels is further divided into eight time slots using TDMA. TDMA and GSM systems increased the capacity by roughly three to four times over analog FDMA systems, which could support only one user per individual channel without interference.

CDMA uses a completely different approach in that every transmission is spread across the same frequency or channel. To make this work without all users interfering with each other, a unique, seemingly random code is embedded into each unique transmission such that the intended receiver can extract the desired transmitted signal from all others in the channel using this code. Many reports indicated that CDMA could carry more simultaneous users without interference, had a capacity advantage over TDMA and GSM, and was roughly ten times more efficient than analog FDMA systems. However, this claim has never been proven fully in the field.

CDMA is based on spread-spectrum technology. It was developed by actress Hedy Lamarr and George Anthiel during World War II to help submarines communicate secretly with torpedoes (although the Navy never adopted this during the war).[1] The basic approach of embedding a pseudo-random code into the transmission that is accessible by the transmitter and receiver paved the way for many innovations in secure communications. These innovations are used today in both the commercial and military world. In fact, Qualcomm aggressively developed an intellectual property portfolio around CDMA that would later become a major factor in the development paths of 2G and 3G wireless standards.

Figure B.5 illustrates the difference between the three basic access methods.

The Capacity Holy Grail: Shannon's Law

There is a basic physical limit on how much information a given amount of spectrum can carry. This may be quantified by Shannon's Law, which describes a channel's information-carrying capacity in terms of the following:

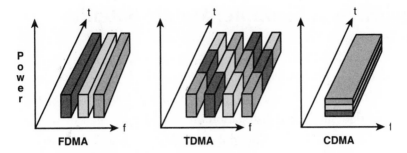

Figure B.5   Comparison of access methods

- The occupied bandwidth (in the case of spectrum, this means how much of it is used)
- The quality of the received signal—specifically, how much of the signal amplitude is above the natural noise floor:[2]

$$C = B \log_2 \left(1 + \frac{S}{N_0}\right)$$

where:

   C = the channel's information-carrying capacity (in bits per hertz)

   B = signal bandwidth, which is how much radio spectrum the signal occupies

   S = signal strength

   N_o = the noise floor (the level of naturally occurring interference)

Shannon's Law could be called the "No free lunch" law. If you go to higher coding or modulation to try to put more bits through the channel, you will need either more spectrum (or bandwidth) or a higher signal level, meaning a high-power, more costly transmitter. Wireless network designers are constantly trading off these parameters based on what the constraint is, such as handset cost, range, or available spectrum. In the case of 3G, 0.3 to 0.5bps/Hz was the system's maximum capacity (not much better than GSM/EDGE), compared to much higher capacities for WiFi and emerging 4G technologies.

Overhyped Example: Mobile Satellite Services

In 1997, a company named Iridium, backed by Motorola and a number of large investors, went public on the promise of launching a leading-edge satellite constellation. It would take on the wireless phone companies by offering global wireless voice and data services anywhere in the world—even on top of Mount Everest. It all made sense, because satellites are the ultimate cell tower. They can cover a much bigger swath than their terrestrial counterparts, as shown in Figure B.6.

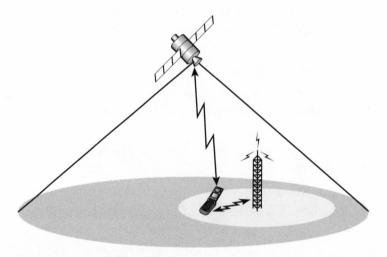

Figure B.6   Iridium satellite phone concept

The lower-altitude Iridium system even promised to cure the "delay" problem experienced previously with calls going over high-altitude satellites. The half-second needed for the signal to get up to the satellite and then back to the ground could be incredibly distracting. Over $10 billion was invested in Iridium and similar systems (Globalstar, Orbcom), with banks like Merrill Lynch projecting a market opportunity of more than $30 billion for satellite-based cellular.[3] But these grand business plans were significantly flawed for several reasons.

One reason was that the phones were incredibly bulky, because they needed hardware and enough power to transmit to a satellite 800 miles (1,280km) in the air. While these phones may have been fine for a user at a home or office, they were unacceptable to mobile business travelers trying to lighten their load. A second reason was the fact that indoor coverage was very poor, because users needed a fairly good line-of-sight signal path to the satellite. An additional reason was that the cost structure of these systems was high due to the enormous expense of building, launching, and operating a 66-satellite system. This required Iridium to charge an enormous premium for the service, especially with a small base of users. The last reason was that GSM and CDMA were beginning to blanket the Earth such that 99% of the places a global business traveler might be (economic zones) had adequate cellular coverage. This allowed the use of small phones at a reasonable price. This left the niche market of hard-to-get-to places like offshore platforms, ships, airplanes, wilderness, and the desert. This remaining market was not nearly large enough to support the bloated global satellite systems. So Iridium and many systems like it went bankrupt, resulting in billions in losses, and giving the satellite industry a black eye in the mainstream telecommunications world.

However, today proven systems like Inmarsat and a restructured and significantly scaled-back Iridium service a fairly profitable niche market of communications for remote location and mobile government users. In fact, Iridium earned $260 million in 2007 from specialty users and is looking to raise $75 million to finance new add-on services to the system.[4] Provided that they are realistic about the limitations of satellite services, they could have a very profitable run.

Can Wireless Be Faster Than Wireline Broadband?

Although it may sound logical that wireless channels would reach the same level of speed as wireline broadband, physical limitations make this nearly impossible. As discussed with Shannon's Law earlier, the speed of a given connection depends on the amount of spectrum or frequency available, as well as the signal-to-noise ratio. As a point of comparison, fiber-optic lines have the most spectrum and the lowest noise level. The signal is transmitted via light over glass, so very little natural interference occurs. Coaxial cable (like your cable TV and cable modem lines) is slightly worse, and copper lines (like your phone and DSL lines) are worse than cable. Both of these media have natural interferers like hair dryers and microwaves that can interfere with the reliable transmission of information over the channel. However, all three of these wireline connections have much higher capacity than a mobile wireless channel, with the same frequency and power level of transmission. Figure B.7 shows the continuous gap when comparing the progression of speeds in residential broadband channels (from DSL to cable modem to fiber) to wireless broadband (from 1G to 4G).

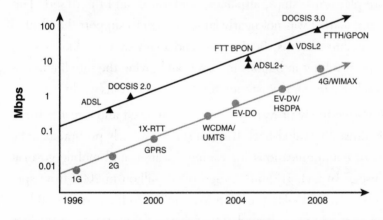

Figure B.7   Comparison of wireless and wireline connection speeds

This is primarily due to the fact that wireless transmits through an extremely variable environment and is susceptible to the following degradations:

- Multipath, in which multiple versions of the same signal collide with buildings and other objects
- Fading, in which the user moves behind objects or away from the transmitter

- Signal path loss due to atmospheric effects (water, smog)
- Interference from other wireless channels

Digitally enabled techniques such as error detection and correction can combat some of these challenges, but they cannot overcome the bandwidth and noise level advantages of wireline connections. Furthermore, the cellular environment comprises many areas of coverage through which the user travels, entering and leaving coverage of the various cells. Intelligent mobility management techniques such as cell selection and handover are used to mitigate the impacts of such user mobility, but these also consume more resources, taking away from bandwidth to the user. The true equalizer between wireline and wireless environments is mobility, which makes the overall convenience and utility of wireless a winner.

2.5G: More Than Just Voice

2G drove an explosion in mobile voice services, but it provided only limited data capability—on the order of 14Kbps or less than a dialup modem at the time. The introduction of and growing interest in the World Wide Web fueled an increasing demand for higher-speed access on mobile devices. While the providers and standards groups were busy laying grand plans for third-generation (3G) wireless to offer broadband services to mobile users, it was still several years away in terms of technology and investment, so an interim solution was needed. GSM addressed this by coming up with General Packet Radio Services (GPRS), with practical data rates up to 85Kbps, and Enhanced Data for GSM Evolution (EDGE), with data rates up to 236Kbps (very close to DSL and cable modems at the time). This required some new equipment to be deployed by wireless carriers and new phones from vendors. But it did not require new frequency spectrum and was not a radical change in their operations given the performance improvement.

In this same time period, Short Message Service (SMS) was taking off in Europe, initially as a low-cost communications alternative to a voice call, and then more as a cultural habit. The same phenomenon would take place several years later in the United States when a new generation of wireless users raised on instant messaging (IM) started using mobile phones.

^RUP^ (Read Up, Please): The Text Revolution

SMS was meant to be just a simple add-on feature of GSM to offer text service in addition to voice. Almost 2 trillion text messages later, this little feature has mushroomed into a universal communications medium across the globe, with its own indigenous language and rules. SMS was commercially deployed in 1993 in Europe. By 2000, it had taken off as a cheap method to bypass the expensive airtime costs at the time. This was particularly true in Europe, where airtime rates are higher than in the United States, and where the calling party pays for the call. (In the United States, both parties pay for the airtime used.) In this case, it made a lot more sense to text someone versus calling him. As SMS was catching fire in Europe and parts of Asia, very little text messaging activity occurred in the United States. The cost benefit of texting was not as significant for U.S. subscribers, so operators in the United States had become much more aggressive with wireless e-mail instead. Figure B.8 shows the overall growth of text messaging in the world versus the United States.

It was not until the burgeoning number of teen subscribers discovered the convenience and immediacy of text messaging that it really took off in the United States. This tipping point was mostly due to the incredible growth of IM prior to 2005 and the growing number of teens with cell phones in the United States. As of 2007, text messaging represented a $100 billion market for service providers, compared to only $65 billion for the sale of all movies, music, and games combined.[6] With the U.S. market finally catching up, text messaging has become a serious medium for both staying connected and expressing yourself around the world. Thousands of unique

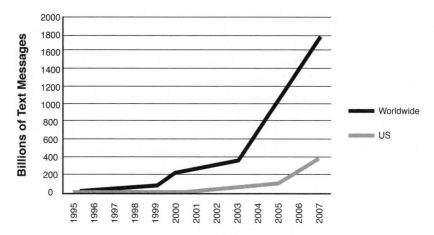

Figure B.8   The growth in global and U.S. text messaging[5]

abbreviations and emoticons have been created to help people express themselves more efficiently through text. But before plunging into the texting universe, make sure you know your stuff, because the differences can be subtle but important. For instance, the difference between yuppie ($-)) and happy drunk (%-)) is just one character!

Bluetooth: Networking All Your Stuff

Many folks don't realize that the Bluetooth standard has been around since 1998. It was aimed at eliminating wires among peripherals like headsets, printers, and music players. But interference, low speeds (less than a typical broadband connection at 1Mbps), and lack of interest limited the growth of the early version (1.1). In 2003, a new version (2.1) emerged with better speeds and quality. The demand for wireless headsets (due in part to growing regulations concerning drivers with cell phones) drove a surge in Bluetooth-enabled devices. Like WiFi, Bluetooth operates on free, unlicensed spectrum. As with any other network standard, the more Bluetooth devices or "networked things" there are, the more valuable the technology is.

Having everything networked also means having everything exposed. And Bluetooth has run into its share of security and privacy issues as a result of its pervasiveness. Because Bluetooth naturally scans for and interacts with any other Bluetooth devices within range, normally about 10 meters, unsuspecting users can be exploited without their knowledge if their Bluetooth connections are left open. Many of these attacks already have names like Bluebugging, Bluejacking, and Bluesnarfing, the last of which involves grabbing information from an unsuspecting user's phone. Using this technique, a few mischievous MIT students hiding behind a tree were able to download Paris Hilton's address book from her mobile phone as she walked out of the Grammy Awards. I am sure it was an interesting list, to say the least! Yet despite these vulnerabilities, Bluetooth has carved out a significant niche in the personal area networking (PAN) market. The recent increase in connection speeds will help Bluetooth better support the demand for transferring larger files and multimedia.

Barriers to the Growth of 3G

Outdated Performance Targets

When 3G standards development started in 1998, residential broadband penetration in the world was relatively low. Speeds typically were in the 256 to 284Kbps range for DSL and cable modems. As a result, the reference point for 3G was to design a system that offered 128Kbps to moving cars, 384Kbps to mobile pedestrians, and 2Mbps to fixed users. As fixed broadband penetration continued to advance around the world, speeds above 1Mbps became commonplace and made a target like 384Kbps seem obsolete. In reality, 3G was unable to deliver even the target levels of performance due to unexpected wireless performance issues following launch.

As 3G failed to meet the increasing thirst for speed, High-Speed Packet Access (HSPA) was introduced to enhance the performance of existing GSM-based cellular systems. This offered the potential for much higher bandwidth for an individual user (in excess of 7Mbps), but at the expense of reduced capacity for other voice and data users.

As a result, carriers are rolling out HSPA carefully in their existing service areas and are developing HSPA+ to increase the speed and improve the overall capacity per cell.

Intellectual Property Ownership

By moving to CDMA as the technology platform for 3G, IP and licensing costs became a significant issue. Only a few companies, like Qualcomm and Interdigital, owned a significant share of the necessary IP for Universal Mobile Telecommunications System (UMTS) (over 256 related patents). This meant paying several dollars in royalties per handset and significantly more for base stations that used Wideband CDMA (WCDMA). In 2007, Qualcomm and Ericsson (one of the largest UMTS equipment providers and royalty payers) reached a settlement to resolve the IP/royalty dispute. However, licensing costs remain an issue for 3G devices. This was a major factor in the Chinese deciding to develop their own standard, SC-TDMA. In addition, the CDMA standard requires GPS for timing. The Chinese government did not want to be in the uncomfortable position of giving the U.S. government the power to turn off its cell phone network! However, the Chinese 3G standard has been delayed several times as they found themselves scrambling for a wireless broadband solution for the Beijing Olympics in the summer of 2008. They ended up relying on 2.5G technologies to bridge the gap. (This fallback strategy allowed Chinese carriers to offer decent speeds for watching multimedia coverage of the events and capture significant data and voice roaming fees during the 2008 Games.)

WiFi Disruption

The unexpected growth of WiFi was discussed earlier. But what wasn't mentioned was the crippling effect that WiFi had on the roll-out of 3G and its perceived benefits. The impact starts with the disruptive economics. Because the bandwidth is higher (11Mbps and greater versus less than 1Mbps), the spectrum is free (except for the supporting broadband access charge, if any). And an access point costs hundreds versus hundreds of thousands of dollars. Therefore, WiFi can achieve a much lower cost per bit transmitted. Based on 2006 performance levels, this comparison was $3 per megabyte for 3G versus $0.02 per megabyte for WiFi. The drawback of WiFi had always been lack of coverage versus cellular. But as hot spots have become ubiquitous in public areas, offices, and homes, that disparity has been diminished. Many users seek out hot spots to get the higher bandwidth and lower cost (if not free). Now that Skype and other VoIP providers offer mobile versions of their service (like Pocket-Skype), WiFi is also attacking the 3G voice market in addition to just data. Any calling taking place within a WiFi hot spot can be sent through WiFi at zero incremental cost over the broadband access itself. This is not something the carriers anticipated when 3G was on the drawing board and they were shelling out billions for licenses.

One carrier saw the early signals of WiFi disruption and went on the offensive. That was T-Mobile, the wireless arm of Deutsche Telkom. It bought access rights to key public areas such as airports and train stations. It cut deals with top retailers like Starbucks, Barnes & Noble, and others to play both sides of the war. Instead of offering a "best-effort" service like WiFi typically provides, T-Mobile sought to provide a higher-quality managed experience that would cater to high-end mobile professionals. Other carriers sneered at this strategy as being a money loser. Meanwhile, T-Mobile is the leading hot spot provider in the United States. It can give customers a seamless experience by offering handsets that support roaming between WiFi and 3G and offering generic wireless access (sometimes called Unlicensed Mobile Access [UMA]). This gives users the benefit of browsing at high speeds and no-cost voice over IP when in range of a hot spot. And they can still access the broader coverage of cellular when WiFi is unavailable.

Lack of Compelling Applications

So where is the killer app? That is what a lot of carriers were asking after the initial rollout of 3G. Other than faster web access, no other real bandwidth grabbers were being heavily used. Promising apps like networked gaming and mobile TV were still relatively nascent when 3G was being deployed. You could argue that some of this was having devices that could render a rich interactive experience. Even in Japan, where it appears that the 3G race is in hyperdrive between NTT DoCoMo, KDDI, and Softbank, customers are not necessarily using the 3G network for rich broadband applications. The majority of traffic is downloading ringtones, simple games, and cartoon character clips (like Pokemon).

The 3G Race in Japan

In recent years, Japan has been called a leader in developing and adopting new electronic gadgets. From the Walkman to portable game players to cell phones, there has always been an appetite for the next cool thing. This is reinforced by the fact that the Japanese spend a lot of time commuting and, therefore, are away from their homes, so mobile devices are essential to both communications and entertainment. Downloading pictures, video clips, games, songs, and other easily shareable media is a big part of the culture in Japan, especially for the younger generation.

To this end, Japan is one of the few markets where 3G has really taken off. Three carriers are in competition: NTT DoCoMo, KDDI, and Softbank. Table B.1 compares technologies, subscribers, and average cost at the end of 2006.

TABLE B.1   Three Competing 3G Carriers

	DoCoMo's FOMA	KDDI	Softbank
Standard	WCDMA	CDMA-EVDO	WCDMA
Peak Data Rate	384Kbps	144Kbps	384Kbps

TABLE B.1　Three Competing 3G Carriers

	DoCoMo's FOMA	KDDI	Softbank
Month Introduced	October 2001	April 2002	January 2005
Subscribers	36 million	27 million	9.2 million
Average Monthly Cost	US$61.11	US$59.82	US$54

The effects of this market have not fully translated to Europe and the United States yet.

While DoCoMo had a significant lead with its 2G offering called i-Mode, this did not translate to success with 3G. KDDI rolled out its own CDMA offering over existing spectrum. The WCDMA offerings of DoCoMo and Softbank required wider channels, and other traffic had to be cleared from existing spectrum to accommodate this.

4G Emerging Technologies

The following sections describe each of these emerging technologies in more detail to give you a basic awareness of their power to change the current wireless model.

Wireless Broadband Networks

3G managed to move the needle a bit on bandwidth (about 500Kbps, or less than half a typical cable modem on average). But the improvements were too little to keep pace with user expectations and the need to support bandwidth-hungry rich-media applications. So in the interim, wireless operators have rolled out patchworks of 3G and "3.5G" capabilities such as HSPA and EVDO, with speeds up to 14Mbps. But these technologies were inefficient patchwork solutions to a larger wave of demand for high-quality mobile broadband services. Users are still unable to get broadband connectivity and internetworking with other users and devices outside of a small set of locations (hot spots) and situations.

Next-generation wireless standards have been on the drawing board since early 2000, but they were given little attention because of the focus on rolling out 2.5G and 3G services. Now that the realization is sinking in that a new solution is needed to service the needs of future users, 4G has gained significant visibility again. The two competing standards are LTE (Long-Term Evolution) and Mobile WiMAX (the IEEE 802.16e wireless broadband standard).

LTE was developed as a next-generation extension of GSM/UMTS. It supports up to 100Mbps downloads and 50Mbps uploads to mobile users. It uses a technology called Orthogonal Frequency Division Multiple Access (OFDMA) and smart antennas (both of which are discussed later) to achieve much higher capacity than 3G systems. Because over 80% of the world uses GSM, they have a tremendous advantage to build on. Even Verizon, which has traditionally used CDMA networks, has committed to LTE as its 4G standard. The standard is still in development, with LTE products expected to hit the market sometime after 2010.

The Mobile WiMAX standard followed a nontraditional development path more similar to WiFi than cellular standards. The initial focus of WiMAX, starting in early 2000, was to create a viable fixed wireless alternative to cable modems and DSL. Something similar to this had been tried previously during the telecom bubble by a number of well-funded, high-profile start-up companies like Teligent and Winstar with proprietary solutions. Even AT&T got into the act with Project Angel, an internally developed fixed wireless approach to combat the Baby Bell broadband offerings at the time. But a lack of standards, reliance on closed proprietary solutions, high equipment costs, and lack of a differentiating value proposition resulted in the failure of these businesses and fueled what was later called "irrational exuberance." The original WiMAX standard was aimed at improving the economics and performance of the previous proprietary approaches by creating an open standard in partnership with key industry players (the WiMAX Forum). The hope was to achieve economies of scale. The original WiMAX standard (802.16a) was issued in 2003. But as the power of mobility became more apparent with the rapid growth of 2G cellular, the WiMAX standards group and industry partners began to develop a mobile version, WiMAX Mobile (802.16e), issued in December 2005.

The basic standard supports mobile wireless broadband at speeds up to 70Mbps across both licensed and unlicensed bands for a wide range of frequencies, providing much more flexibility and deployment options than cellular. However, questions still surround WiMAX's range and ability to manage user handoffs versus more proven cellular-based technologies. With Intel's agreement to put WiMAX chipsets into new laptops, the introduction of WiMAX-capable handsets from Samsung, and commitments by service providers like Sprint, Clearwire, and several international players, WiMAX has the makings of a formidable competitor for future wireless broadband networks. The key will be developing an ecosystem of devices, like cameras and media players, and applications like mobile entertainment and virtual conferencing, that leverage this network.

Table B.2 compares LTE and WiMAX in terms of estimated performance.

TABLE B.2   Comparison of LTE and WiMAX

	LTE	WiMAX
Peak Download Speed	100Mbps	70Mbps
Peak Upload Speed	50Mbps	5 to 10Mbps
Average Range	30+ miles /48+ km	1+ miles /1.6+ km

Given the huge uncertainty in deployment costs and actual performance, it is tough if not impossible to pick a winner. It is possible that a new disruptive solution will come from left field, such as Ultra Wideband (UWB), discussed in a moment, to stake out the 4G opportunity.

OFDMA: The Wireless Capacity Booster

The concept of Orthogonal Frequency Division Multiple Access (OFDMA) has been around for decades. However, the cost of the technology to make it practical in wireless networks and handsets was prohibitive until recently. OFDMA uses Fourier Transforms to pack many more individual wireless transmissions into a given wireless channel with minimal interference.

If deployed over a sufficient amount of radio spectrum (more than about 10MHz), OFDMA can offer even greater spectral efficiency than the other wireless access methods. This capacity gain is statistical in nature, kind of like providing a large pipe through which more information can flow more of the time. This is one reason it offers even greater spectral efficiency than CDMA alone, which is why all the potential 4G standards are using some form of OFDMA. It is also used in several variants of WiFi (802.11a, g, and n).

Ultra Wideband: The Wireless Broadband Wildcard?

Think of Ultra Wideband (UWB) like CDMA on steroids. The technology was developed by both Russian and U.S. researchers. (We're not sure who stole it from whom!) They were working on wideband radar systems that use short electromagnetic pulses to detect incoming threats. Instead of spreading the signal over a traditional wireless channel, UWB spreads the signal over a much wider bandwidth (up to 8GHz wide, or 1,600 times wider than a typical 3G wireless channel!). UWB can use this extremely wide swath of frequency without interfering with other users in the same spectrum. It transmits in micro pulses at a level so low that it is below the noise floor (meaning that it would be indistinguishable from typical noise in another wireless channel). This requires extremely heavy coding and wideband radios to allow the receiver to extract the signal at this low a level. The upside is unlimited bandwidth (in theory), giving UWB huge potential to provide much higher connection speeds than even proposed 4G standards like LTE. The first applications of UWB were short-range wireless networks. This included incorporation into the next version of the Bluetooth standard to provide 100 to 200Mbps for connections from 10 to 20 meters. But expect more aggressive application of this disruptive technology in the future. Chipsets are available for several dollars each and are decreasing in price.

Cognitive or Software-Defined Radios

Early wireless devices were designed to communicate on a specific frequency band using a given wireless standard. Mobile devices then evolved into *multimode*, in which the device could switch to different frequency bands, including switching between analog (1G) systems and 2G systems. Currently, devices on the market can even switch between WiFi networks and other 2G and 3G cellular networks based on the proximity or signal strength of a WiFi hot spot. Looking forward, we expect to see devices that not only can switch between several defined frequencies and standards, but also can operate across a broad spectrum and on a wide variety of wireless standards. This requires flexible radios in the device that can operate across a wide range of frequencies and are configured in software, where each new wireless standard can be downloaded directly to the phone.

The U.S. military does this today with its Joint Tactical Radio System (JTRS). It can handle more than 30 different wireless standards. It operates across a large swath of frequencies so that soldiers, vehicles, and planes can easily communicate versus having to carry multiple radios, as they did in the past. As additional computing power has become available to mobile devices, more intelligent or *cognitive* functions are emerging, as shown in Figure B.9:

- **Spectrum awareness** is the ability to identify and utilize unused spectrum at any given time (because the spectrum may be available only temporarily). A recent NSF study showed that the existing wireless spectrum is used on average only 14% of the time.[7] With frequency-agile devices, existing spectrum

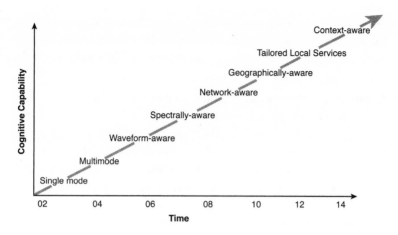

Figure B.9   The evolution of cognitive functions in mobile devices

constraints could be overcome. Different devices would coordinate with each other in accessing available spectrum at various points in time. DARPA has already demonstrated Dynamic Spectrum Access (DSA) for military applications, in which troops may have to adapt on-the-fly to available frequencies, depending on where they are in the world. If the operators and regulators can come together to develop comprehensive guidelines for DSA, we could see it become more prevalent in the commercial environment with 4G networks.

- **Network awareness** is the ability to detect all available networks and select the one that will provide the optimal cost performance for a given application. For example, an e-mail may not need a low-delay network. But a video feed would be degraded significantly, so the user may be willing to pay more for access to this network for an important videoconference. This means that the radio must be able to both identify available networks and determine what quality of service (QoS) is available on each network. It must also be able to exchange user authentication information for billing and management.

- **Geographic awareness** is when the device knows exactly where it is. It can use this information to help the user make decisions about the availability and proximity of services, for example. It might know where the closest hotel or restaurant is.

- **Tailored local services** is the ability to use geographic information to tailor specific applications such as education or entertainment that are related to the user's specific location. An example would be having the voice of Ben Franklin start providing facts on historic sites on your phone as you walk through Philadelphia.

- **Context awareness** is essentially augmented reality (AR). The user's specific situation is determined, such as knowing he is running based on his heart rate and location. Then useful applications are provided based on this information, like buzzing the user's phone and presenting statistics on his running performance, and maps of possible routes and distances from where he is.

Cognitive radios, possibly more than any other 4G technology, have the potential to disrupt the wireless services business model by putting the user, not the carrier, at the center of the network. This will resurface when we talk about possible future scenarios for 4G.

Moving from Hardware to Software

If you want speed, the traditional answer has always been to design functions directly to hardware, or to "hardwire it." If you want flexibility, the answer has always been to put it into software so that functions can be easily updated. However, performing a given function in software (like authenticating a user with a cell tower) on a general processor generally is always slower than if the function were designed into a chip. In addition, general processors or CPUs have traditionally been more expensive than Application-Specific Integrated Circuits (ASICs). But as Moore's Law has continued unabated, computing power has become very small and very cheap. It's to the point where software running on CPUs is fast enough to perform some of the heavy, complex functions in radios operating on several different networks. Figure B.10 shows a standard radio and a software-defined radio in which much of the specific hardware has been replaced by a wideband front end and a general processing back end.

By putting more functionality into software, the device becomes much more powerful in the scheme of wireless networks because it

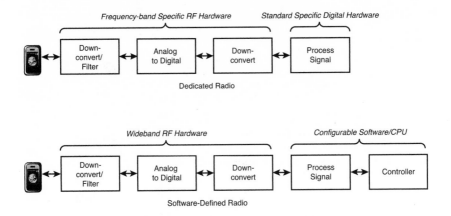

Figure B.10   **Software-defined radio versus a dedicated radio**

can now choose the best option across many networks. This may not be ideal for the wireless operators, who become more commoditized "pipes" as users gain more control of which networks they communicate over.

Smart Antennas

Earlier in this appendix, frequency reuse was mentioned as a key fundamental concept in cellular systems. In addition, the quest to move more bits through a given wireless channel is one of the major objectives in 4G. Smart antennas offer benefits to both frequency reuse and data rate in a given channel. Smart antennas that are adaptive can refocus their antenna elements to create different-shaped patterns, as shown in Figure B.11.

Today's systems primarily use simple omnidirectional antennas (meaning they essentially transmit and receive signals in all directions) on the handsets and omnidirectional or sectorized antennas on the cell towers. Sectorized antennas divide the cell into slices served by a specific antenna to increase the frequency reuse. Also, suppose I could dynamically shape the antenna's patterns based on the location

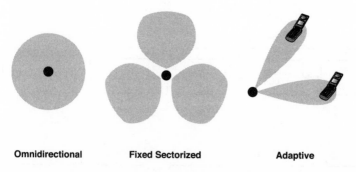

Omnidirectional   **Fixed Sectorized**   **Adaptive**

Figure B.11   Comparison of antenna patterns

of users within a cell at any given time (think about a spotlight following an actor across the stage). The capacity of the overall cell could be
increased dramatically, and the power required for each handset
could be reduced. So having an antenna pattern directed at specific
users is an enormous benefit when you are trying to conserve precious
battery power in the handset and reduce interference among users.

Additional techniques are being used as part of 4G systems, such
as using multiple antennas to transmit the same information in parallel to improve overall performance.

Increasing the number of antennas to transmit more information
in parallel is also an opportunity to increase performance. Most of the
4G systems being proposed incorporate an approach called Multiple
Input Multiple Output (MIMO) antenna designs to maximize connection speeds.

The Power of Multiple Antennas

MIMO antennas are ones in which both the transmitter and
receiver use multiple antenna elements to break up and transmit
parts of the communication stream in parallel. Increasing the number
of elements on both ends directly increases the channel's capacity in
proportion to the number of elements. Most systems deployed today
are Single Input Single Output (SISO) and follow Shannon's Law for
the maximum possible channel capacity. Some recent MIMO systems

have shown a dramatic 400-fold capacity increase over 2G systems and a 40-fold capacity increase over 3G systems. This means 40 times the number of conversations or data transmitted, increasing the range of services and overall revenue potential for these systems.

Putting a lot of antenna elements on the mobile handset could be very costly. An interim approach is to put multiple antennas on the base station and transmit the same signal multiple times with a single antenna on the receiver. This is called Multiple Input Single Output (MISO). It improves the channel capacity by a factor proportional to the log of 1 plus the number of antenna elements times the channel's signal-to-noise ratio.

Figure B.12 shows the different antenna configurations, from SISO to MIMO.

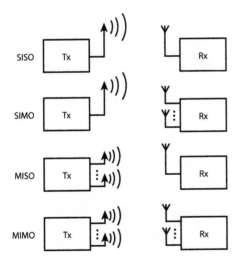

Figure B.12   SISO, SIMO, MISO, and MIMO antenna configurations

Mesh Networks

Mesh networks, sometimes called Mobile Ad hoc mesh Networks (MANETs), are a completely different approach to wireless networks than traditional cellular networks. They differ from a very structured cellular layout with hub-and-spoke communication, in which each

mobile user must communicate via the cell tower/base station to connect to any other user. Mesh networks allow users to connect directly
to each other. They also use other users as "relays" to reach their ultimate end user. In many ways, the users *are* the network. This is much
like peer-to-peer networks for file sharing (such as Kazaa and eDonkey), where users operate without a central management authority
based on open standards. The "ad hoc" part allows users to form and
dismantle these networks at any time based on need. Figure B.13
illustrates the basic difference between cellular networks and mesh
networks.

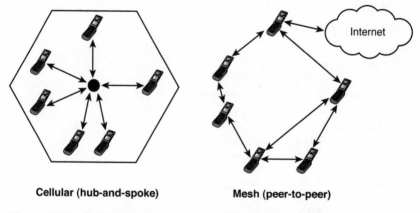

Cellular (hub-and-spoke)   **Mesh (peer-to-peer)**

Figure B.13   Cellular versus mesh network configurations

The U.S. military has been one of the lead developers and users
of MANET due to its unique requirements for battlefield communications. Both the network nodes and end users are constantly changing in terms of visibility, range, and ability to communicate. This
means that the network must be constantly updated to meet users'
specific needs to communicate with each other at any given time. By
allowing different assets to communicate directly with each other in
real time, the U.S. military has reduced its "sensor-to-shooter" time
(how long it takes from detecting a threat to launching an attack)
from three days to 5 minutes. So from the time a soldier identifies a

nearby threat to the time a Predator Unmanned Aerial Vehicle (UAV) launches a missile at the target, you may just have enough time for a cup of coffee!

More recently, commercial applications of mesh networks have started to emerge:

- **Surveillance/monitoring**, where moving platforms like buses or even people can relay information to other moving platforms about their situation or environment.
- **Office networks**, where mobile users within an office can quickly configure a network to communicate with each other and even have one user become the access point to the Internet. Greenpacket is an example of software that allows each laptop or mobile device to act as a router for others.
- **Internet access relays** such as Fon, where each user is a router and relay in a large-scale network to provide shared Internet access at a low cost or even for free with the equipment.

A number of practical challenges still exist for the commercial use of the MANET concept, especially concerning the power consumption of very small devices. For example, would you really want someone draining your battery power if your phone is used as a relay for someone else's messages? What economic incentive might you need to allow this? These are some of the questions that must be considered as MANET migrates into more mainstream applications.

These applications are enabled by the fact that the basic cost paradigm is completely different for mesh networks versus traditional cellular networks. In capital-intensive cellular systems, infrastructure represents 80% of the overall system cost, whereas mobile devices are only 20%. In mesh networks, the model is flipped, with infrastructure representing only 20% of the cost and devices being 80%. Devices must contain significantly more intelligence to act as both end-user terminals and routers or access points for the overall network. This allows mesh networks to be deployed rapidly and in stages as needed.

A number of major cities in the world, like Taipei, have deployed mesh networks with over 2 million nodes in them. And they have done this at a fraction of the cost of a traditional cellular or point-to-multipoint broadband network. Where no infrastructure currently exists or where it is too difficult to install towers, mesh networks can be an ideal solution. Challenges exist, though. If not enough users are in close enough proximity to each other, gaps could exist in the coverage. Also, too many users can cause performance to degrade due to the large number of hops required, as shown in Figure B.14. This must be taken into account when a mesh network is designed to make sure the user requirements can still be met, even at the degraded level.

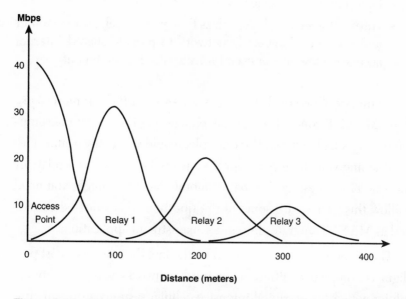

Figure B.14   Signal degradation in mesh networks from multiple hops[8]

One of the other big challenges in mesh networks is that any node can talk to any other node, making it very difficult to distinguish a legitimate user from a malicious one. Bluetooth, discussed earlier, is a type of ad hoc network that allows different nodes to quickly make connections and form networks with each other. This opens its associated security vulnerabilities, also discussed earlier. (WiFi can also be configured to operate in ad hoc mode.) Due to its somewhat biological properties (self-forming viral connections), malware can spread like an epidemic through these networks. Users are slowly waking up to the security issues associated with open ad hoc connections and are starting to think before making their device visible to all networks. 4G networks will need to overcome this issue if users are to have access to mesh networks in the future.

Taking on the Phone Companies with Fon

Fon was started by Argentinean entrepreneur Martin Varsavsky in 2005 with the goal of creating a global wireless network using users' WiFi broadband connections. The basic value proposition is that users would be willing to share a portion of their wireless broadband access to other Fon users (called Foneros) in exchange for having access to hot spots of other Fon users as they roam. They could join Fon by purchasing a Fon access point/router and then having free access when and where it is available. Much like peer-to-peer file-sharing networks, the Fon network needs lots of users to provide enough coverage to make it attractive to most users. Despite $55 million in venture funding and high-profile backing by BT and Google, there were still less than 1 million Foneros worldwide as of mid-2008. This made the coverage very spotty compared to other alternatives. Competitors include "hot spot" providers like T-Mobile and Boingo. They try to offer hot spots in high-traffic areas like airports, hotels, parks, and other public places where Fon coverage is less likely to exist. Meanwhile, Apple has been deploying WiFi routers that can link Apple users in a network that could be very similar to Fon. The question is, how will these ad hoc mesh networks compete with the other 4G alternatives coming down the line? Or will they coexist with networks like Fon given more cost-effective options for users than just traditional wireless operators?

Wireless Sensor Networks

In 2007, 10 billion microprocessors were sold and embedded into everything from computers to coffee makers. Machine-to-machine (M2M) communication accounts for more traffic than all human communication combined. Figure B.15 shows the expected M2M traffic in the next several years.

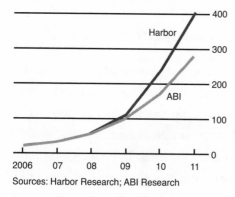

Figure B.15   Projected growth in machine-to-machine communications[9]

Some projections have the number of connected objects reaching 100 billion in the next decade! Much of this massive nonhuman communication is being driven by monitoring and control applications. Sensors relay information to other nodes to interpret and then make decisions based on the updated information. Examples of this type of sensing and control include everything from home energy and heating control to security systems and environmental monitoring. Even the thousands of mousetraps at Wembley Stadium have been connected via a wireless sensor network (WSN) that relays the status of each trap (closed or open). This way, maintenance workers can save significant time by going to only the traps that have been tripped.

The objective of WSNs is to connect dispersed sensing nodes to relay critical information to decision-making nodes as reliably and efficiently as possible. Most WSNs use an ad hoc approach, as discussed previously, where nodes can self-form communications. For example, suppose you air-dropped a number of sensors in the forest to sense potential fires before they spread. The specific locations and spacing of the sensors will be irregular, so they will need to find each other and then determine the most efficient routing paths for data through the network. One node acts as the access point for the entire network.

Target applications for WSNs include monitoring the following:

- Heavy machinery components to determine if they are degrading or need replacement
- Tire pressure to reduce tire wear and improve overall mileage
- Local temperature of overheating components or fires
- Local atmospheric data to track and project weather events
- Chemical/biological/nuclear (CBN) scans to detect hazardous levels
- Traffic monitoring at distributed points to inform traffic routing
- Tracking first responders to coordinate emergency response efforts

Here are some of the challenges in effectively deploying WSNs:

- **Power**—Sensors tend to be highly distributed, which means that they require a long-life remote power source (battery or other).
- **Size/aesthetics**—Sensors are often integrated with other parts or appliances and, therefore, must be small enough to integrate into even small components.
- **Disposal**—Leaving expired sensors in the field pollutes the environment.

For a number of years, sensor networks were based on proprietary standards and, like RFID, failed to achieve economies of scale. In late 2005, the Zigbee Alliance was formed to create an open flexible standard for WSNs. Zigbee focused on some of the big WSN challenges by developing a lower-power approach. It supports up to

10,000 sensors, transmits up to 100Kbps, and conserves battery power to last three to five years per sensor. Although other options exist for networking sensors cheaply, Zigbee strikes the ideal balance of range, power management, and reliability.

Companies like Ember and Millennial Net have leveraged Zigbee to create a comprehensive set of residential and business WSN applications like intelligent building monitoring and control. In addition, a large number of mainstream chip vendors are producing low-cost Zigbee chipsets to achieve greater scale. Like GSM, Zigbee is proving that open standards can provide a significantly greater growth opportunity if well managed.

Location-Based Services

Location-based services (LBSs) have emerged by adding the dimension of location on top of wireless communication networks. Location information comes from one of two methods—Global Positioning System (GPS), which uses satellites, or Time Difference of Arrival (TDOA), which uses cell towers to determine the user's location. The need for location information originally was driven by the need to control users in CDMA systems. It also was driven by E911 (Emergency Location Services) requirements levied on wireless carriers so that distressed users could be located when they called 911 on a cell phone. But recently, this location capability has spawned a whole new wave of LBS applications expected to result in over $3 billion in revenue in the next few years. One example is TrackMyPizza.com, where customers can track the delivery status and location of their pizza order using the driver's GPS-enabled cell phone. Another example is a wildfire warning system in Contra Costa County, California, where citizens get alerts if they are in an at-risk area based on their mobile device location. Figure B.16 shows the future projection of LBS revenues.[10]

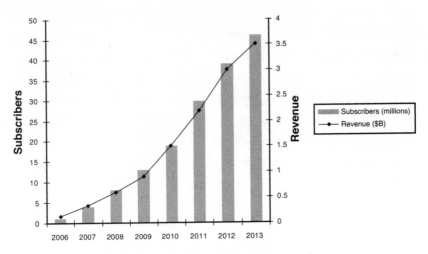

Figure B.16 Projected growth in location-based services revenue

With the emergence of free and open-source mapping applications using the Geographic Information System (GIS) framework like Google Maps, the availability of mobile user location information provides lots of opportunities to create new services. These include real-time traffic updates, shopping guides, and even touring information. Casinos like Harrah's have even applied LBS to track casino chips as they move through the casino to track betting patterns at different tables. OnStar is a more well-known example of LBS. A driver's location can be used to give her guidance on how to get immediate service or maintenance, and value-added services. Coupled with cognitive devices, LBS has the potential to offer a true suite of "concierge" services for mobile users.

Pinpointing the Location of Mobile Users

GPS uses at least 24 satellites in medium Earth orbit (MEO) about 12,000 miles (19,200km) up. They determine the position of a given user by triangulating his signal from several satellites, depending on how many satellites are in view of the user. GPS was originally developed to support the military in tracking the location of soldiers and assets and to guide weapons to their targets (like precision guidance of cruise missiles). Accuracies were as low as 1 meter by using time and position information from each satellite broadcast on two frequencies, L1 and L2. As civilian applications appeared, the U.S. Department of Defense agreed to make a commercial version of the L1 signal available for devices at a degraded level of accuracy of about 100 meters; this was called selective availability. Eventually the DoD agreed to make the undegraded L1 signal available for civilian applications. This allowed much better accuracies in the 5- to 10-meter range when supplemented by other reference ground-based sources. (This is called differential GPS.) The military still encrypts the L2 signal for its own use. Figure B.17 shows how the location of different users (airplane, car, and ship) are calculated using the GPS constellation. If you are an oil company positioning a drill ship or an airplane trying to perform an assisted landing, GPS is mission-critical to your operation's success or failure. It will become more so with consumer and business wireless applications in the 4G future.

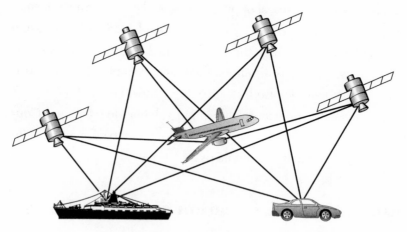

Figure B.17   GPS navigation overview

An alternative geolocation method for mobile users is Time Difference of Arrival (TDOA), which uses the signals of cell towers to triangulate where the user is. Because cell towers are on the ground and the GPS satellites are 16,000 miles (10,000km) in the air, the level of accuracy is much less for TDOA—about 15 to 30 meters. But this is still sufficient to meet E911 requirements. Figure B.18 shows an example of TDOA location for an E911 call.

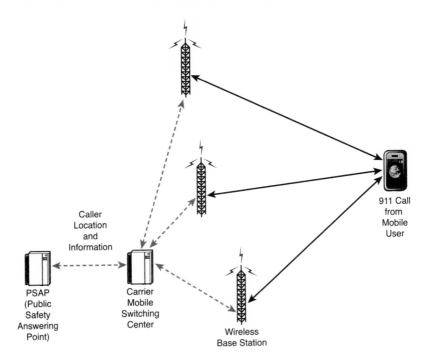

Figure B.18   E911 call using TDOA

Because all CDMA handsets already have GPS chipsets, and many GSM/3G handsets also have GPS chipsets, most users today can achieve the higher accuracy associated with GPS to support emerging location-based services.

Endnotes

Introduction

[1] Sterman, J. D. (2000) *Business Dynamics: Systems Thinking and Modeling for a Complex World*, Irwin/McGraw-Hill.

[2] Schoemaker, Paul J. H. (2002) *Profiting from Uncertainty: Strategies for Succeeding No Matter What the Future Brings*, The Free Press.

[3] Christensen, Clayton M. (1997) *The Innovator's Dilemma*, Harvard Business School Press.

[4] Van Putten, Alexander B. and Ian C. MacMillan (2008) *Unlocking Opportunities for Growth: How to Profit from Uncertainty While Limiting Your Risk*, Pearson Education, Inc.

Chapter 1

[1] *Guide to Community Engagement Marketing*, February 2008, swarmteams white paper (www.swarmteams.com).

[2] Rheingold, Howard (2002) *Smart Mobs: The Next Social Revolution*, Basic Books, pp. 157–8.

[3] *40 Years of IT: Looking Back, Looking Ahead*, IDC special edition executive white paper, 2004.

[4] Burrill, G. Steven. "Biotech 2007: A Global Transformation," Nov. 19, 2007, UMBI presentation.

[5] Key Global Telecom Indicators for the Telecommunication Service Sector, ITU 2007.

[6] *Wi-Fi HotSpot Forecasts*, ABI Research, third quarter, 2008.

[7] Various research reports (Instat, WiFi Alliance).

[8] *WiFi Equipment Forecast*, Primedia Research, 2003.

[9] Strategis Group Forecast of 3G Mobile Subscribers, 2000.

[10] "Pass the Painkillers," *The Economist*, May 3, 2001.

[11] Decision Strategic International 3G Revenue Estimate, 2006.

[12] Informa Telecoms and Media Estimate, December 2008.

Chapter 2

[1] Rheingold, Howard (2002) *Smart Mobs: The Next Social Revolution*, Basic Books.

[2] Hesseldahl, Arik. "There's Gold in Reality Mining," *Business Week*, March 24, 2008.

[3] "Living in a Connected World," *The Economist*, Special Supplement, 2007.

[4] NHIS 2003-6, Neilson Mobile Midyear Estimate for 2008.

[5] Blue, Laura. "World of Warcraft: A Pandemic Lab?", *Time*, August 22, 2007.

[6] Rifkin, Jeremy (1995) *The End of Work*, G.P. Putnam's Sons Publishing.

[7] Prahalad, C. K. (2006) *The Fortune at the Bottom of the Pyramid*, Wharton School Publishing.

[8] International Telecommunications Union (ITU) Statistics, 2007.

[9] Christensen, Clayton M. (1997) *The Innovator's Dilemma*, Harvard Business School Press.

[10] Sterman, J. D. (2000) *Business Dynamics: Systems Thinking and Modeling for a Complex World*, Irwin/McGraw-Hill.

[11] Schoemaker, Paul J. H. (Winter 1995) "Scenario Planning: A Tool for Strategic Thinking," *MIT Sloane Management Review*.

Chapter 3

[1] Kurzweil, Raymond (2005) *The Singularity Is Near: When Humans Transcend Biology*, Viking Press.

[2] Tapscott, Don (2008) *Grown-up Digital: How the Net Generation Is Changing Your World*, McGraw-Hill.

[3] Rheingold, Howard (2002) *Smart Mobs: The Next Social Revolution*, Basic Books.

Chapter 5

[1] Cisco white paper, "Wireless Solution Enhances Florida School District's Administrative and Classroom Services," 2005.

[2] Heim, Kristi, "UW Team Researches Future Filled with RFID Chips," *Seattle Times*, March 31, 2008.

[3] "Wireless Technology for Social Change: Trends in Mobile Use by NGOs," United Nations Foundation and Vodfone Group Foundation, 2008.

[4] Executive WiQ Survey, Snyder, 2007–8.

[5] Ibid.

[6] Ibid.

[7] Bennigson, L. A. (1996) "Our balkanized organizations." *Planning Review*, 24(2), 38–40, Program Planning.

Chapter 6

[1] Day, George S. and Paul J. H. Schoemaker (2006) *Peripheral Vision: Detecting the Weak Signals That Will Make or Break Your Company*, Harvard Business School Press.

[2] Van Putten, Alexander B. and Ian C. MacMillan (2008) *Unlocking Opportunities for Growth: How to Profit from Uncertainty While Limiting Your Risk*, Pearson Education, Inc.

[3] Day and Schoemaker.

Chapter 7

[1] Commuting in America III: The Third National Report on Commuting, Transportation Research Board of the National Academies, October 16, 2006.

[2] Motorola white paper, "Wirelessly Connecting the Dots: Mesh-enabled architecture solutions for intelligent transportation systems" (2005).

[3] National Heart Lung and Blood Institute Statistics, 2007.

[4] Ibid.

Appendix B

[1] Mock, Dave (2005) *The Qualcomm Equation*, AMACOM.

[2] Saadavi, Tarek N., Mostafa H. Ammar, and Ahmed El Hakeem (1994) *Fundamentals of Telecommunication Networks*, John Wiley & Sons, Inc., p. 51.

[3] Pioneer Consulting Satellite Broadband Forecast, 1999.

[4] Iridium Corporate Information (2007) revenue and new capital raise.

[5] ABI Research Forecast 2008.

[6] Ibid.

[7] McHenry, M. and D. McCloskey, "Multiband, Multi-location Spectrum Occupancy Measurements," Proceedings of the International Symposium on Advanced Radio Technologies, Boulder, CO, March 7–9, 2006, pp. 167–175.

[8] Tafazolli, Rahim, editor (2005) *Technologies for the Wireless Future*, Wiley, p. 343.

[9] Harbor Research, ABI Research, Forecast of Machine-to-Machine Communications, 2007.

[10] Frost and Sullivan Forecast for Location Based Services, 2008.

INDEX